GW00374124

Easy Gardening

with

THE CHEAP LAZY GARDENER

by

ARABELLA MAY BIDDLE & LAUREN BURLINGTON

www.thecheaplazygardener.com

©2006 Magnificat Productions Ltd

COPYRIGHT:

The right of Arabella May Biddle and Lauren Burlington to be identified as the authors of this work has been asserted in accordance with sections 77 and 78 of the Copyright Designs and Patents Act 1988.

Easy Gardening with The Cheap Lazy Gardener
By Arabella May Biddle and Lauren Burlington

Copyright © 2006 Magnificat Productions Limited

ISBN 0-9553146-0-7
        978-0-9553146-0-5

Publisher:
Magnificat Productions Limited
Suite 243, 405 Kings Road, London SW10 0BB, England, United Kingdom

Cover Design: Ivy Forsyth
Book Design: Vesna Petkovic, Neslie Hollinshead
Production and Editing by: Natgraphics / V. Yankovich

Copyright under International and Pan-American Copyright Convention.
All rights reserved, including the right to reproduce this books or portions thereof in any form, except for the inclusions of brief quotations in a review. The text of this book, or any part thereof, may not be reproduced or transmitted or distributed in any form by any means, electronic or mechanical, including photocopy, recording storage in an information retrieval system or digitally rendered or otherwise, without the written permission of the publisher, Magnificat Productions Limited.

Neither the Publishers nor the Authors can accept liability for the use of any of the materials or methods recommended in this book or for any consequences arising out of their use, nor can they be held responsible for any errors or omissions that my be found in the text or may occur at a future date as a result of changes in rules, laws or equipment.

TABLE OF CONTENTS

4	Acknowledgements
5	Introduction
7	Cheap Lazy Starters' Planting Snapshot
11	The Cheap & The Free
16	Cheap Lazy Easy Does It
20	Cheap Lazy Water Ways
24	Cheap Lazy Ponds
27	Cheap Lazy Plant Power
32	Cheap Lazy Lawns & Lawnmowers
36	Cheap Lazy Composts
37	Cheap Lazy Classic Cottage Garden Choices
39	Cheap Lazy Animal Magic
42	Cheap Lazy Pest & Weed Control
47	Cheap Lazy Pots & Containers
50	Cheap Lazy Cacti & Succulents
51	Cheap Lazy Low Maintenance Hardy Plants & Trees
54	Cheap Lazy Top 50 Favourite Plants
59	Cheap Lazy Top 10 Clematis - Top 5 Cut Flowers
60	Top 10 Easy Care Tough Plants
62	Cheap Lazy Vegetable Garden Snapshot
65	Cheap Lazy Tree Snapshot
68	Cheap Lazy Herbs & Their Uses
71	Cheap Lazy Childrens' Choices
73	Cheap Lazy Disabled Extra
76	Cheap Lazy Spirits of Place
79	Cheap Lazy Language of Flowers
83	Cheap Lazy Last Word (or so)
87	The Cheap Lazy Gardener Has the Last Laugh
88	Cheap Lazy Birthday Flowers
89	Cheap Lazy Plant Spells and Love Potions
95	Bibliography

CHEAP LAZY ACKNOWLEDGEMENTS

All sorts of people from all sorts of places have contributed to this book. Notably we would like to acknowledge substantial help from Denise Howell without whom the book would never have got beyond a great idea at The Castle one Sunday. Myriad corrections were picked up by our gifted editor, Gail Tinsley of Darkcat Press in Goleta, California. Any that escaped her eagle eye are the result of extra material being fitted in up until the last possible moment! Bill Le Grice and Liz Barnes of Rosebuddies at Wroxham Barns in Norfolk were unstinting in their expert help and encouragement on many fronts. Hermione Young and Denise Lee gave us both our first and our best testimonials so far: the boost from those was a real tonic when we needed it.

Geli Bartlett of Victoria BC, Canada weighed in with horticultural expertise of the highest order, and Vesna Petkovic of ProArt in London made sure that we eventually made it to market. Jayne Lawton of Grobox is joining with us on various ventures; Sue Coyle of the Clydesdale Bank gave us encouragement and financial backing to put this all together, and Alex Griffiths and Mona Wara have put together a website so the world can check it all out, from anywhere, anytime **(www.thecheaplazygardener.com).** Talk about modern miracles!!

Thanks are due to all the above and many more: errors are ours. If you find any, please let us know: if you like the book, please tell **_all_** your friends!!

This book is for my father, Sir Steel Pasha, Pasha of pashas, Lord of the Western Islands and Penders, master of Castle Felix, whose _joie de vivre_, love of nature and sense of fun infuse life with happiness; in memory of my grandparents, whose loving kindness, courage and firm principles always held true in an uncertain world; for my family and friends, who make life worth living; and for Magnificat herself.

Magnificat Productions

CHEAP LAZY INTRODUCTION

Savour the look on your friends' faces as they see you relaxing and enjoying your free, *easycare* garden! Save your time and money with over 365 of the world's best gardening secrets and top tips. In this easy little guide you'll uncover new ways to make use of what you already have, and if you don't have anything yet, it will provide you with enough information to start a garden for virtually no cost and in next to no space.

What do you want in a garden? Indoors or outdoors? Do you think of just a pot, some herbs on your windowsill, or rolling acres of beautiful flowers and velvet lawns? Eating delicious fresh vegetables straight from the vine? Gorgeous trees and shrubs, something for the children or grandparents? Chilling on your patio after work, or looking out of the window at your collection of lovely ceramic pots filled with greenery?

How can you create what you want without years of hard work and spending a fortune? Start here! Our objectives are simple: top tips to save you time and money, and fresh, beautiful and organic results, not hard labour or heavy expenses.

Cheap is pretty much the first thing we look for. How can you achieve what you want for free? Or at least for the tiniest possible cost. We just hate to part with money if we can avoid it. Recycling has a lot going for it, and someone else doing the work is even better. Or going further and creating beautiful areas that need no work at all.... well, that takes us to another priority.

Lazy is our other byword. If there's a way that doesn't involve effort or strain, an easy, lazy way, then that goes straight onto the list. Fun goes along with easy, of course: the point is to get more enjoyment out of life with less hard work, and smaller financial outlay, naturally. Timesavers of all kinds are top, so once you've made your garden beautiful and organic, you'll free up more hours and money to enjoy it, doing whatever you like best.

Organic tenets are always uppermost in our minds. Sometimes they include methods which are cheap but not necessarily lazy, and some which are lazy but not necessarily cheap. We've also included some items just for general interest or for their beauty, and some for children and the disabled, for gardens nourish everyone.

These gardening facts, hints and tips have been gathered from friends and neighbours, amateurs and professionals alike who care for gardens great, small and in-between around the globe. Some solutions we've discovered on our own, inspired by the example of the many marvelous gardening books, publications and clubs. Our experience will save you time and money, making gardening easier, cheaper and organic, minimising the use of conventional gardening products, or just using things in a different way to help your garden bloom for you.

CHEAP LAZY STARTERS' SNAPSHOT

Many of these topics and ideas are touched on throughout this guide - but here is a snapshot of what first to consider and assess when you are **starting from scratch.**

Have you got some space to garden? If not, you could probably share with someone. Check to see if your community center or municipality runs an allotment program. If so, you could probably rent some ground for a very modest fee. In some places, local residents are growing flowers and vegetables completely for free in patches alongside disused railroad tracks or other derelict land. Allotments run at around £23 ($37) each per year. Joining a gardening club is always good value - the cost of membership will give you the key to a whole new world of interesting people as well as fantastic advice and bargains!

Alternatively, consider setting up a mini-garden on your balcony, or inside on a table or shelf, or even the ceiling. You can successfully put a plant in a hanging basket, a tin can or even a bottle or old fishbowl. Any of these can produce very satisfying and productive results in the most restricted space: begin with a grow bag or a couple of pot plants and experiment to see what suits you.

Always **check the toxicity of plants** before you buy or grow. Some are poisonous to **cats, dogs, horses, birds** and **people**, so make sure you know for certain that they are safe before you take them home or put them in the ground. Also make sure that the plants you choose are legal for your area: devastating pests and diseases can sneak in all too easily.

Climate, light, soil type, plant placement and availability are all key factors which you should look into in planning a garden. Sunny and dry is a world away from rainy and damp: different plants thrive in different places. If you check these out and plan accordingly you will save time, money and effort and avoid disappointment. Some suggestions follow:

Placement:

Sun: Poppies, roses, cacti, sunflowers, marigolds, cape daisies, love-in-a-mist, Black-eyed Susan, petunias, lavateria.

Shade: Euonymus, vinca, ivy, evergreens, spring bulbs, hostas, begonias, busy lizzies.

Dry shade:	Olives, oleanders, nerines, sternbergias
Part shade:	Lilies, clematis, camellias, azaleas, pieris, peonies, bluebells, periwinkle, fuschia, honeysuckle, sarcococcas, skimmias.
Ponds:	Oxygenating, marginals, water lilies, floating plants, those for water features and edges of ponds, faery moss, star grass, spiral rush, bog bean, parrot feather, water hyacinth, reedmace.
Wet soil:	Iris, lobelia, bog marigold, grasses, ferns, astilbes, ligularias, hydrangeas.
Dry soil:	Lupins, bearded iris, Echinacea, ceanothus, pinks, lavender, rosemary, sage
Windy:	Buddleia, cornus, willows, conifers, hebes, grasses, gorse, phormiums, cordylines, pines
Sloping:	Ground cover shrubs or grass, conifers.
Clay:	Shrubs, day lilies, phlox, peonies, spring bulbs, bedding plants.

Check the zone map for your area for the suitability and hardiness of your proposed plants. In Europe go to **www.gardenweb.com**, which gives 10 different zones. In Canada check the Department of Agriculture and Agri-Food Canada on **http://wms.1agr.gc.ca**. In the USA go to the United States National Arboretum site **www.usna.usda.gov** for information.

Run through this check list in relation to your ground and proposed plants:

*Aspect of garden (north, south, east, west) and climate conditions.

*Ph level (acidity/alkalinity) ie for azaleas and rhododendrons, blueberries, etc.

*Nutritional balance (nitrogen, phosphate, potassium, iron etc.)

*Integrated pest management

*Biological controls

*Disease resistance

*Nutritional balance

*Color combinations and textures and sizes of plants

Here are some more plant ideas to consider:

Plants for Sun:

Alpines:	Acaena (various), Arabis, Dryas, Leontopodium, Aurinia, Cerastium, Iberis, Thymus, Saxifrage.
Bedding:	Petunia, Mesembrythemum, various Helichrysum.
Perennials:	Sedum, Cineraria, Dimorphotheca, Lupinus, Lychnis, Phlomis, Helichrysum, Physalis, Gypsophila, *Nepeta 'Dropmore'*, *Nepeta 'Six Hills Giant'*, Artemesia, various Anaphalis, *Hollyhock Alea 'Summer Memories'*.
Shrubs:	Various Artimesia, Azara, Atriplex, Ballota, Cortaderia, Convulvulus, Ceratostigma, Corydyline, Caropteris, Doryenium, Euonymous, Eleagnus, Genista, Hippophae, Helichrysum, Lavatera, Lavendula, Lippia, Olearia, Phlomis, Perovskia, Pittosporu, Rosmarinus, Ruta, Santolina, Salvia, Senecio, Teucrium, Ulex, *Viburnum plicatum 'Summer Snowflake'*, Yucca.
Trees:	Eucalyptus, Robinia, Caragana, various Acacia.

Plants for Wet Soil:

Flowers:	*Iris pseudocorus* (Flag Iris), *Lobelia cardinalis 'Queen Victoria'*, Astilbes, *Caltha palustris* (Bog Marigold), *Mimulus luteus* (Monkey Flower), Ligularia, Lysichiton (Skunk Cabbage), Hostas turtlehead *(Chelone glabra)*, cardinal flower *(Lobelia cardinalis)*.
Grasses:	and ferns such as *Osmunda regale* (Royal Fern).
Trees:	Salix (Willow), Alnus(Alder), Taxodium (Swamp Cyprus), Sambucus (Elder), *Rheum palmatum.*
Shrubs:	*Viburnum cassinoides* (withe rod viburnum), buttonbush *(Cephalanthus occidentalis)*, *Clethra alnifolia* (sweet pepper bush), *Cornus racemosa* (grey dogwood), *Cornus*

amomum (silky dogwood), *Cornus sericea* (red osier dogwood), *Ilex verticillata* (common winterberry), *Myrica pensylvanica* (northern bayberry), *Physocarpus opulifolius* (common ninebark).

Notes:
Improving drainage can help your plants survive and thrive. Try raising planting soil an inch or so above the surrounding surface with good quality soil and organic fertilizer. Alternatively dig shallow drainage channels around the outer edge of plants or planted areas to help surplus water drain away.

Mulching in winter will protect against frost and cold. A couple of inches of compost or manure help achieve this.

Water loving plants are **hungry feeders** so give them a boost with some fertiliser in the spring.

Availability will vary enormously from area to area, country to country and continent to continent. If the exact variety you would like is not available or too expensive or wouldn't work out, then check out others. There are loads of different types of roses for example, or conifers: or different types within the species, ie. pine trees, daffodils, snowdrops, etc.

A garden really lives only insofar as it is an expression of faith, the embodiment of a hope and a song of praise.

Russell Page

THE CHEAP AND THE FREE

Old car tires with a piece of glass or plastic on top make good **cold frames**. They absorb heat, insulate against cold, and keep moisture in, providing perfect conditions for seedlings.

Save ice cream and popsicle sticks and plastic knives to use as garden **labels**, or cut them out of old plastic containers of different colors for color coding. Use pencil if you want to re-use the labels, or else use ballpoint ink or waterproof felt-tip markers.

Create free protectors for young plants by making from clear plastic bottles - if they're made of glass and cost more than £25 ($50), they're called cloches. Cut off the dark bottoms and place the clear tops over the plant, leaving the caps off to ensure ventilation. Cloches keep pests off and guard seedlings against sudden frosts.

Recycle food trays from your supermarket to grow plants from seed: they're just the right depth. To save work further down the line, fill them with cores from toilet paper or paper towel rolls (cut these in half), fill each tube with about three quarters of an inch of sharp sand for drainage, top up with compost and sow the seeds directly. Make sure you use new seed compost. Then when the plants are bigger you can plant them easily straight into the ground: as the cardboard decomposes it adds fiber to the soil. Fruit and vegetable flats work really well too if you want to set up lots of seedlings.

Make your own tonic spray from chopped up onion or garlic bulbs. Soak them overnight in cold water, together with a few cloves and some chamomile flowers. Spray your plants liberally to increase their resistance to **pests and diseases.**

A **block of oasis** cut into 2" squares makes an ideal cutting hoilder. Make a hole in the center of each square and insert your cutting. Stand the blocks in a tray of water: the oasis will only take up the amount of water it needs, thereby preventing the cutting getting water logged and rotting. When roots appear through the oasis, pot the cutting in the normal way. You can also use this method for sowing large seeds such as sweet corn or marrow.

Coffee grounds, which contain about four per cent nitrogen, one per cent phosphorus and three per cent potassium, provide a perfect source of **fertile organic matter** for plants.

Clean stone paths and garden statues easily — just pour water that's been used to cook potatoes over them, rinse - and hey presto! No scrubbing at all.

Give new pots or statues an aged, verdigris look quickly and easily by rubbing them with plain yogurt that contains active cultures. (It will state if active on the yogurt container.)

If your **lettuce** is bolting faster than you can eat it, give the plants a shock to slow their growth. Dig them up and leave them in the shade for an hour or so; then replant them. They will take several days to adjust, saving your harvest for your salad bowl.

Getting a haircut? **Human hair** contains many minerals and trace elements that are beneficial to plants. Ask your stylist to keep the clippings for you and mix them into the soil when you plant, an easy and free organic booster.

Grandma used to sprinkle crumbled mothballs on the soil to protect against **carrot fly**. These days we know that the two major ingredients of mothballs are toxic, so try lavender oil instead.

A few small pieces of charcoal placed in a bottle garden or terrarium will help keep the soil sweet and **prevent algae** build up.

A cheap and easy cleaner for **plastic garden furniture** may be made by mixing baking soda and water into a paste and applying. Let it sit for a few minutes before wiping it off and rinsing.

To make **compost** - a natural organic fertiliser, mix garden waste, lawn clippings, leaf mould and vegetable scraps etc in a home-made box in the garden and leave to decompose. This can be done even in limited space, and takes roughly from 6 weeks to a few months.

Grow varieties of plants that require **little staking** close to each other for mutual **support.**

To produce good leaf mould, collect as many leaves as you can, put them in black plastic bag, moisten them - but not too much - and close the bag with a plastic or wire twist tie, compressing the contents. Make a few holes in the bag with a garden fork or pitchfork and store the bag over the winter in garage or shed or somewhere sheltered. Next spring you should have great organic leaf mould, which gardens love.

A **recycled compost bag** makes a cheap alternative outdoor hanging basket . Empty the bag and fold it inside out, then fold over the top a few times and refill the bag with compost. Make holes on each side near the top and attach a string handle. Secure the top with clothespins, then slit the bag's flat side(s) and insert the plants. Make two small holes in the bottom for drainage. Hang the planter up, then remove the clothespins and water the compost. The plants will soon fill out to hide the bag.

For completely **free fruit** and **vegetables**, grow your own from the seeds of what you eat. That bunch of grapes could turn into a vineyard and the orange in your lunch box often has seeds enough for a whole grove. Peppers are filled with seed, tomatoes, cucumbers, melons, olives, apples & pears. Avocado pits are seeds too. Your weekly food shop could grow you a grocery-full! Note that not all seeds are fertile, so you may need to plant a good few for results.

Use new, unused disposable diapers or panty liner to line inside the bottoms of **hanging baskets** - the gel absorbs water and works like the expensive gel crystals at a fraction of the cost.

Ask your greengrocer or produce manager for the **compressed paper separators** used in apple boxes to keep the fruit from bruising. Soaked for an hour in warm water, they can be molded to line hanging baskets. They last a season and are easy to plant through: they're also free and environmentally friendly.

Old blankets can also be used for lining hanging baskets. Thrift shops or jumble sales are good sources.

If you don't have a spreader for **dry fertilizer** etc., use an old coffee jar. Drill holes in the plastic lid, fill the jar with fertiliser, and shake as and when required.

Banana skins placed around **rose bushes** will rot down and provide beneficial nutrients. Try two banana skins per bush in the growing season.

If you don't have any **tools** - borrow them or make do. Forks, spoons or chopsticks might be all you need, depending on the size of your garden. Alternatively consider buying one and sharing with a co-gardener in exchange for using one of theirs, etc.

Instead of paying high prices in the larger gardening centers and nurseries look out for bargains in your **local and regional newspapers.** All year round they advertise bulbs etc., at a fraction of the price of most gardening centers. (Ensure they are suitable/legal for your area.)

If you have a shady garden or one that is often damp, then a variety of hardy ferns would be ideal for your situation. Ferns provide an interesting contrast of greens and shapes, they look spectacular in containers, and they're sensational when planted in gravel, pebble or stone beds or with ornamental grasses.

Try some hardy *Astelia chathamica* in a shady spot: just add some humus to the soil. *Millium effusum 'Aureum'* (which seeds around and comes true from seed) and *Elaeagnus angustifolia* (Caspica group), better known as quicksilver, also work well.

Blues and purples don't show up well in the shade, so plant bright red, orange, yellow and white flowers there instead.

By the sea *Elaeagnus ebbingii* is not only a great value, it's also ideal as a windbreak. *Salvia argentea*, arctic summer *(Verbascum bombyciferum)* and blue haze *(Acaena microphylla)* are also good bets, as are any of the sea hollies. And then there's thrift, which is both cold hardy and heat resistant—a true friend to the cheap and lazy!

To add year-round interest to your garden for very little money, make some mobiles or wind chimes out of anything weatherproof: old flatware, shells, small bits of broken china, and pieces of wood or pipe are universally accessible. If you don't want much noise, don't use metal or string your creation so that nothing hits its neighbor. If you like random sounds, choose your materials and stringing methods accordingly.

Kitchen gardens work hard to produce your harvest. Repair some of the wear and tear during the autumn and winter by sowing red clover, which acts as living mulch and prevents the soil's valuable nutrients from draining away. A legume, it also fixes free atmospheric nitrogen. Sow the seed as if you were sowing grass seed and rake gently. After a slow start in the autumn, growth will halt through the winter. In early spring the clover, which produces an array of brilliant red flowers, will grow to approximately 12 inches. Wait until the flowers start to die off before mowing, then leave the cuttings on the soil surface for a few days to wilt. Dig it all in to provide a top organic booster for your next crop.

If you protect your plants during the winter, you won't have to replace them the next year: how cheap and lazy can you get? Bubble wrap and garden fleece are our first choices—staple to secure them—but old newspapers make a very good, free second best. Straw works too.

Creating different levels in a garden can be fun as well as utilitarian. Add interest by building up beds using bricks, old railway ties, rocks, wooden crates and boxes—all fairly available and sometimes free. In China rocks have been an integral part of garden design since at least 206 BC, and represent the mountain element in landscape - which shows the tradition has a long heritage! Demolition sites are good sources of materials, as are wine and interior design shops, freight depots, shipyards and retail outlets that receive crated merchandise.

Keep your eyes open for interesting junk that might enhance your garden. One friend painted several old car tires, stacked them up and topped it all off with an upside-down garbage can lid that served as a birdbath. They make a great fences or planters too, as well as the time-honored swing for the kids.

Reflective surfaces add dimension to your garden. Cover a board with aluminum foil and prop it behind some plants to see if you like the effect. Spray the board with a metallic paint alternatively. This also works to liven up containers.

Should you have an allotment in inner London UK, Her Majesty the Queen will supply and deliver manure free of charge, delivered by truck to your allotment in the early morning subject to the routines of the palace stables. Enquiries to the Head Gardener in the Royal Potting Shed via Buckingham Palace on 020 7930 4832.

For other English gardeners, check the website set up by RJ Harris, Head Gardener of the Tresillian Estate near Newquay, Cornwall, for a database of free horse manure sources at www.moongardening.fsnet.co.uk.

Commercial rhubarb forcers are expensive. Save money by placing a pot at least 18 inches deep (cover any drainage holes) or a bucket placed upside down over the crown of the plant.

Check out your local dollar or pound shop for excellent garden offers. It's amazing what you can get for just a dollar or a pound. The quality is often excellent.

A garden is the fairest field for the imagination, in the endless combining of forms of novel beauty.

Edgar Allan Poe

CHEAP LAZY EASY DOES IT

The laziest possible garden is a fake landscape. Artificial everything is widely available and represented very realistically. This is pretty much a one off cost, just wash down or replace from time-to-time, no worries about pests. Try **www.fake.com** if this appeals to you.

If you have a very **small garden** but like to sit outside in the summer consider gravelling, paving, decking or laying down astro turf to the most part. Inject some interest with containers of varying shapes and sizes filled with flowers, shrubs, and even fruit and vegetables such as strawberries or tomatoes.

If that's more than you want to do, but you also want some color, buy **colored pots** and fill with a variety of low maintenance grasses and shrubs.

If you can't afford some of the more exciting pots in the garden centers, buy plain ones and get the children to mosaic or **paint some**. Color, fun, variety and art education in one!

Get someone else to do the work. You may know some folks in apartments who would just love to get out into a garden and grow something. Try your local community center or mall and post a notice. **Swap** a day or two's gardening each week against a share of the vegetables or flowers or maybe something else you have to offer, work, produce or whatever. Work less and meet new people!

Barter work for plants too. Hold a regular garage **swap shops** and exchange cuttings or seedlings with your neighbors. This gives you all the chance to try out new things for free, and probably get some great tips on what works or doesn't work as well in your neighborhood or what suits certain plants.

Get the **children** involved - most children will love to have a small patch of herb garden to grown their own produce or alternatively if you have a large area and children make a large sandpit for them. Make sure it has a lid for rainy days. It is also very useful for your bulbs, which can over winter in it. Also children will be more apt to eat what they've grown themselves.

Add variety to your garden and **avoid** any potential **back injuries** by growing plants and vegetables in raised beds. Keep these to reasonable sizes and plant densely to keep weeds at bay. Around six feet square works well and allows access to all parts of the bed.

If you have thin soil or tough conditions, then save yourself a lot of time and money by making sure you choose plants to suit. There is a huge range of cacti for **desert areas**, and for places prone to drought try dune grasses, lavender and santolinas. Some great silvery plants include Eli blue, one of the *Festuca glauca*, and the textural *Ballota pseudodictammus* as well as *Helichrysum petiolaris*. The Sonora desert native yellow morning glory *Merrimia aurea* is heat resistant and will grow 20 feet or more in a season.

For **shady spots** try *Astelia chathamica* which is really hardy, but needs some humus in the soil, *Millium effusum 'Aureum'* (which seeds around and comes true from seed) and also Quicksilver, *Elaeagnus angustifolia* (Caspica group).

Try a **fruit trees** in containers. You will find that their fruit is very frequently tastier than the full size version. Choose the compact varieties. Make sure you use a deep container at least 15" in diameter. Easy pickings!

Avoid overdoing things. Being so exhausted you can barely move after a hard day's weeding definitely takes away the pleasure, so don't go mad. Garden **little and often**, to increase your enjoyment and avoid strain.

Save yourself going back and forth to the tool shed or garage - keep everything you need about you in a gardening apron, with handy pockets. A toolbox or alternatively a bucket will do.

Save hours of **digging**: let Mother Nature do the work for you. To keep your soil in good condition, an initial cultivation followed by a thick annual organic dressing, is more than sufficient. If you are able to do your digging in winter and live in an area where you have frost but not solid ice, then the frosts will help in breaking down large clods of earth, making the digging a huge amount easier. This is a good time to dig in well-rotted manure too - gradually - not too much at one time! Next year's plants will thrive, not just survive.

Rotate crops such as mustard and clover both to add vital nutrients to the soil and to keep diseases from taking hold.

Reduce the number of high-maintenance herbaceous plants in your garden and opt instead for mixed planting, using a selection of shrubs that **don't need hard pruning.**

Bare soil is bad news. Mother Nature abhors a vacuum and she'll take over as quick as winking an eye. The solution? **Ground cover**. For best results plant a single type, whether alpine, perennial or shrub. Some of our favorites are: periwinkle, saxifrage, thyme, acena, ceratium, epimedium, euphorbia, catmint and Rose of Sharon. Rubus pentalobus (crinkle-leaf creeper) provides year-round ground cover and is tolerant of all sites. Gravel, paving or decorative stone for weed control, organic mulch for feeding, and trouble-free ground-cover plants to cover every inch, will give you the upper hand.

Banish those formal, **labor-intensive**, annual bedding schemes in favor of great swathes of colorful hardy annuals that you can sow direct in minutes. Also try *Geranium macrorrhizum, Geranium 'album'* or *Geranium x cantabrigiense 'Biokovo'* planted en masse for low maintenance, *Euphorbia characias, Euphorbia amygladoides var. robbiae* (Mrs. Robb's bonnet, spurge), *Geranium rozanne, Geranium 'Johnsons blue'* and *Astrantia major* (masterwort) which blossoms over 5 months for virtually no effort.

Reduce the number of bulbs, such as tulips and dahlias that need lifting every year, and be more liberal with those that don't. Pick varieties that will naturalize easily, to **colonise large areas over time.**

Ordinary tar-oil winter wash takes the hard work out of lifting **moss** from paths and driveways at a fraction of the cost of proprietary cleaners. Apply it with a pressure sprayer, leave to dry and then simply sweep it all away.

Replacing hedges with **low-maintenance fencing** will put an end to all that trimming. If you do prefer a hedge, choose trouble-free beech, holly, yew or berberis - they only need a quick annual trim.

Try growing bush tomatoes - they're just as good as the cordon varieties, but without the extra hassle of **staking, de-shooting and stooping.**

When you've boiled eggs, use the leftover water to pour between the **cracks** in the **path** to prevent weeds growing. Organic and free!

Weeds - when hoeing the ground, only disturb the top 1/2" of soil. Going deeper than this will cause more weed seeds to germinate.

Heating - Place a few garbage bins filled with water under greenhouse staging. The water will heat up during the daytime, releasing warmth and humidity slowly at night. Concrete flooring in greenhouses will also store heat from the sun and provide similar benefit.

Got a **vacant spot** and can't decide what to grow in it? Whilst you are making up your mind, sow some hardy annuals in it. They will help break up the soil and provide a welcome splash of colour. They also attract beneficial insects, which will help keep the pest populations down and of course provide flowers for cutting. Furthermore, many will self seed and so provide copious seed for subsequent years.

Trying to keep back the tide of weeds is an ongoing battle. There are many products on the market that do this admirably but they are expensive. Bark, gravel, coloured stones & specialist sheeting etc all can rack up the costs especially if you have a large area. We have a cheaper version. Keep all your old newspapers. When weeding move about 1" to 2" (5cm) of earth, lay down say 3 to 4 sheets and cover the ground. Move the earth back over it and it will inhibit the weed growth very well. We use newspapers as they are biodegradable and cost you nothing. Or if you rather like your weeds but still find them choking or invading certain plants then just bury your newspapers around the area surrounding those plants.

Nature does not complete things. She is chaotic. Man must finish, and he does so by making a garden.

Robert Frost

CHEAP LAZY WATER WAYS

The **Amazon river** contains more water than the combined volume of the next eight largest rivers in the world.

In general, water little but often. If you have a small garden, use a long-spouted watering can with a fine rose to ensure even water distribution and prevent damage to your plants. None of them wants a pounding or a drowning.

Stop watering **strawberries** when the fruit turns from white to red to reduce the risk of grey mould fungus. Once you have picked the fruit, the plants will start producing baby plants on long stems. These can be pegged down into the soil or a small pot, and once they have rooted you can cut them from their parent to produce separate plants.

Placing a piece of wood upright in a plastic **water barrel** will prevent the barrel from splitting when the water freezes.

Lay an irrigation hose, or an old hose with holes pricked out at regular intervals, just under the soil at the back of the borders to save time when watering your garden. Just leave the tap on for 10 minutes as necessary. This saves not only time and money, but a possible soaking.

If automation isn't for you, mix SwellGel in with your soil as directed. The phostrogen releases moisture when and as the plants need it. This is especially useful for container plants.

Line **runner bean trenches** with torn-up newspaper. It retains moisture and cuts down on watering.

Use a long **rain stick** to water hard-to-reach pots and hanging baskets: no more trying to balance on a wobbly chair or ladder.

Never use water collected from water barrels to water seedlings. Use tap water, but allow it to stand for an hour or so to allow the chlorine to evaporate.

Use a **cork on a bamboo cane**, or a tap container with a knife handle, to test whether a potted plant needs watering. If the plant is thirsty, the pot will ring like a bell when it's tapped; otherwise, you'll hear a dull thud.

Mix **Perlite** and/or SwellGel in with the compost when preparing patio planters and hanging baskets. It absorbs water and releases it when the compost is dry.

Tomatoes grown in slight salty water have been shown to taste sweeter. A teaspoonful of salt dissolved in two gallons of water applied once early in the season should do the trick. Be sure you water regularly to avoid the tomato skins splitting if the fruit swells too rapidly after being deprived.

Before filling a **strawberry barrel**, stand a piece of drainpipe or cardboard tube up the middle and fill it with pebbles. As you add the soil, gradually remove the tube to release the pebbles. This forms a central drainage system, preventing the soil from becoming waterlogged.

Hanging baskets need watering twice a day when the weather is extremely hot. Ice cubes, which release moisture slowly as they melt, may be placed in the baskets, but ensure that they do not touch the plant because this could cause damage. To make it easier to lower and raise pots and baskets, hang them from a pulley rather than a hook. Lee Valley in North America supply a very good version.

Hang your garden hose on an **old wheel rim** mounted in the garage or on a wall. Your local wrecking yard should have plenty to spare.

Hanging baskets, planters and pots dry out much quicker than the garden, so line them with black garbage bin liners before you fill them (remember to leave the drainage hole clear). Once you've potted your plant, lay some glass marbles, pebbles or aquarium gravel on top of the soil to further retard moisture loss.

If drought strikes you will want to keep your garden growing, but there may be a ban on hose use in your area. It is quite safe to use **recycled water** from the shower, bathtub or dish basin on lawns and borders, but avoid using any water containing strong detergents or bleach, which could not only damage plants and soil but contaminate the ground water.

Don't overwater. Once the risk of frost has passed, the plants you've started indoors may be safely moved outside. Water them thoroughly to settle the soil around their roots, but in the following weeks water only if the ground is very dry. Too frequent watering prevents roots from developing strongly and retards the plants becoming self-sufficient with strong growth.

If you have a **greenhouse**, sprinkle water over the floor whenever you can to raise the humidity. This will reduce the plants' demand for water overall.

Use a dry watering can to apply fertilizers such as bone meal exactly where they're needed. You won't have to bend too much, you won't be scratched by any thorns, and you won't breathe in obnoxious dust or other particles.

Make sure your watering can is not too heavy for you when it's full. The plastic versions are much lighter than the metal. If you need to reach hanging baskets, tall pots or pots on high shelves, buy one with an extra long spout.

If you're a busy or frequently absent gardener, an **automatic drip watering system** might prove ideal. These systems, which are switched on and off at the tap either by hand or on a battery-operated timer, connect pots, planters and/or hanging baskets along a thin hose. You can water your plants without lifting a finger!

Keep **wooden containers** from drying out by lining them with plastic. Make sure the plastic is perforated to allow for drainage before filling the containers with soil and plants.

To minimise waste water gently at the **exact point** where the plant needs it. A dripper nozzle attached to thin black tubing achieves this, with or without an automatic watering system.

To **reduce moisture** loss through evaporation from the surface of the ground around both your pot plant and garden plants, cover it with perforated black plastic. Cover this in turn with gravel, which reflects light, keeping compost cool and moist. Vine weevils are also kept at bay, as it's difficult for them to lay their eggs under these conditions.

Wood chip mulch is also very effective at holding back weed growth as well as maintaining temperature and keeping in moisture. We recommend wood chips because they gradually decompose, adding nutrients along the way.

A **seep hose** with a porous skin to soak the soil directly by your plants or a dripper nozzle, also helps keep weed germination to a minimum.

Water from your rain barrel is ideal for **acid-loving** plants.

Remember, however, that water stored in such containers can go stale over time. Use a product like *Refresh* to keep it sweet and clear. Keeping the containers covered prevents mosquitoes breeding.

If your water is **metered** you will save money by using water saved from your bath or shower for your plants. This is easier on the environment too. Bonus: a slightly soapy solution will also deter aphids. (Remember that strong detergents etc. will damage plants.)

One of the best ways to save on watering is to plant for drought. Tough plants thrive on skimpy soil and can be left to fend for themselves to a remarkable degree. Try old favourites rosemary and lavender. Others to consider include pelargonium and artemisia and of course basil, chives, comfrey, and mint. Take a bit of care with mint: it can be incredibly invasive and is best in a container. Vetiver helps bind the soil and gives a nice texture, and for the long term there is nothing more satisfying than an olive tree.

All gardening is landscape painting,

Alexander Pope

CHEAP LAZY PONDS

To create a pond, dig a hole the size and shape desired and line it with concrete or rubber, an appropriate plastic or butyl. Make a shallow shelf about a foot wide at the sides of the pond for plants that like shallow water, then drop the pond a couple of feet in the center to allow for water lilies or floating plants such as water hawthorn. If this sounds too intimidating you might consider buying a pre-formed rigid plastic or fiberglass shape, but remember that it's not going to be cheap.

Concrete

This is a two-step process. Be certain to work with fresh, properly prepared cement for best results. Using a mixture composed of 3 parts by bulk washed gravel, 1 part builder's sand and 1 part cement, make the first layer 2 to 3 inches thick. Start with the bottom and then build the sides. Bear in mind that the cement will usually be workable for about a maximum of three hours. Once this is firm enough to walk on but not fully set, add a second layer, also 2 to 3 inches thick, made of a finer mix of 1 part cement, 3 parts builder's sand and [How much?] waterproofing liquid or powder, again starting at the bottom and building up. Paving slabs or rocks may be used to conceal the raw edge of the concrete if desired; allow them to hang over by an inch or so. Fill the pond with water and then empty it once or twice before stocking to make sure any harmful impurities are washed away. This is hard work and time consuming, but it's pretty cheap.

Rubber plastic or butyl

Make sure the sheet of lining is large enough to cover the bottom and sides of your pond and leave a good overhang at the top. Then do a final check to ensure there are no stones or other sharp objects in the prepared bed. Smooth it over with the back of a spade and cover the whole surface and up the sides as much as possible with an inch or so of sand. Place the sheet in position and press it down to follow the contours of the bed, holding it in place around the top with bricks or rocks a few inches from the edge. Then fill the pond with water. The added weight will settle the sheet onto the base, drawing in its edges a bit. Trim the edge of the sheet between 6 and 12 inches around the margin and bury it under turf, paving or rocks to secure and conceal it. This doesn't require as much hard work as the concrete method, nor does it take as long, but it is more expensive.

Preparation of ponds for planting
Either cover the bottom and sides of the pond with good loamy soil covered with about an inch of clean gravel or sand and plant prior to filling with water, or build up mounds where planting is intended holding in place with fine mesh netting. Alternatively plant into baskets filled with soil and sink the baskets in position where desired.

Cheap, Easy Alternative Water Features
Sink an old bathtub, half a barrel or a bucket into the ground and surround it with pots of varied heights and plantings. Add a reasonable depth of soil and sand (around three or four inches) plant as desired and fill with water.

Line halves of wooden casks or kegs for use on patios. These make great water lily features.

Plants for ponds
The best time to stock a pond is the spring. We suggest starting with the following plants:

• Deep water plants:
Canadian pond weed, English water violet, Water hawthorn, Umbrella grass *(Cyperus longus)*, Pond Weed *(Elodea crispa* and *Elodea densa)*, Water Poppy *(Hydrocleys nymphoides)*, Water Milfoil *(Myriophyllum verticullatum* and *myriophyllum spicatum)*, Water Lilies (ie. *Nymphaea alba, Gladstoniana odorata, Helen Fowler, Albatross, Escarbouche, James Brydon, Rose Arey, Graziella, Sunrise)*, Floating Heart *(Nymphoides Vallisneria spiralis)*.

• Shallow water plants:
Sweet Flag, Water Plaintain, Giant Reed, Flowering Rush, Bog Arum, Marsh Marigold, Kingcup, Sedge Grass, Cotton Grass, Iris, Rushes, Mint, Bog Bean, Monkey Flower, Water Forget-me-not, Arrow Arum, Pickerel Weed, Arrow Head, Bulrush *(Scirpus tabernaemontani zebrinus)*, Reed Mace, Cat-tail.

• Bog Plants:
Astilbe, aconitum, cimicifuga, hemerocallis, lythrum, lysimachia, podophyllum, rodgersia, saxifrage, trollius, dodecatheon, primulas, bamboo, willow, alder, taxodium, gunneras, rheums, ferns *(Osmunda regalis)*.

During **hot summers** keep an eye on your pond and make sure you keep the water level topped up. This helps **add oxygen** to the water and keeps your fish and plants in good health. Fountains and pumps are a good idea to help keep the water from going stagnant.

Birds, frogs, insects and wildlife will benefit from ponds and water features too. Birdbaths and decorative fountains further extend the idea. A huge range are available very reasonably, or can be created easily for free. Solar powered lights, pumps and filtration units make it possible to build water features into any corner of any size garden.

A garden is the purest of human pleasures. It is the greatest refreshment to the spirits of man, without which buildings and palaces are but gross handiworks.

Francis Bacon

CHEAP LAZY PLANT POWER

Poor planting brings poor results, so make sure you follow the instructions on each flowerpot label. Be sure to space your plants properly and plant them at the right depth in the right soil: otherwise you'll be replacing them before you know it.

Check that the plant you have your eye on will do well where you want it to grow. Planting a shade-loving plant in full sun, or a sun-lover in deep shade, is a recipe for disaster. **Always choose the right plant for the right place**. It'll save you a great deal of time, trouble and expense in the long run.

Running out of **space**? Grow runner beans up sunflowers for a pretty and practical solution. Sow the sunflowers early in the season, so they're about a foot high when you plant the beans. By the time the beans start climbing, the sunflowers will be the right height and have enough strength to support them.

Study plant labels carefully before buying anything. Look for words such as **"hardy" "compact"**, **"evergreen" and "long-lived"** to ensure a cost-effective, easy-care garden.

"A rose is a rose is a rose." Choose easy-going **shrub roses** that need little attention, or modern compact, free-flowering rose varieties with good disease resistance. Decide if you're going for looks, scent or both before you buy.

Team naturalizing **spring bulbs with ornamental grasses** such as *Holcus mollis 'Albovariegatus'*, *Lagurus ovatus*, or *Carex elata 'Aurea'*. Once the bulbs have bloomed, the emerging foliage of the grasses will disguise their yellowing leaves.

Include some plants especially for **winter.** Mahonia looks great year round, but in winter it produces lovely sprays of deep-yellow flowers scented like lily of the valley, and then navy-blue berries as well.

More winter blossoms. *Prunus subhirtella Autumnalis* as a delightful cherry-blossom substitute. *Viburnum bodnantense Dawn* blooms through December, producing lots of frost-proof pink flowers and, like the elusive *Viburnum tinus 'Spring Bouquet,'* requires no maintenance to speak of. *Lonicera x purpusii* (winterflowering honeysuckle) is fragrant from November until March and is an easy, most accommodating plant.

Irises in December are another great joy, and they will grow happily in terrible soil as long as have enough sun. We suggest you try the Algerian native *Iris unguicularis*, which goes on for weeks and weeks, and *Clematis cirrhosa Freckles* and Purple Universal pansies to lighten gray winter days. Aconites such as the bright yellow *Eranthis hyemalis* herald the start of the year in January.

Winter beddings, including white cyclamen and skimmian ssp reevesiana, complement evergreen plantings. *Euonymus fortunei 'Emerald Gaity'* (wintercreeper) is a grand background through the winter, and *Helleborus x hybridus* flowers from January on.

If you want **scent in your winter garden**, consider the gorgeous winter scented Daphne, Witchhazel, which has a spicy perfume and wintersweet *Chimonanthus praecox* (this takes some years to settle in to flower).

Berries and hips will fill your garden from autumn through New Year if you plant crab apples *(Malus Evereste* or *Malus Red Sentinel), Pyracantha Watereri* or cotoneasters and roses such as *Rosa rugosa* and *Rosa moyesii 'Geranium.'* Bright-stemmed dogwoods such as red *Sanguinea 'Midwinter Fire'* and yellow *Cornus sericeara Flaviramea* also provide a marvellous background. These will save you time and money with your winter decorations - they are immediately to hand and once planted will give you returns year on year.

The more a **chamomile** bed is stepped on, the more it will spread. Chamomile has the ability to revive and improve any plant growing next to it, and chamomile tea has been drunk for centuries as an organic soother.

Pinch the tendrils off of the **sweet pea** plant to promote its flowering capacity.

Resist choosing herbaceous plants, including beddings, just because they are in flower. **Look at the overall plant and condition of the roots**. Choose a plant full of buds in preference to one in full flower as it will go on flowering for much longer.

Watch the way you water. The most likely cause of an older plant's losing its leaves is underwatering. The most likely cause of a younger plant's leaves going yellow is overwatering.

Stop a windowsill houseplant from becoming lopsided by turning it every couple of days. This will also keep it healthy. Try moving your houseplants around too, within their sun and shade requirements.

If you have an orchid whose flowers have died off, so you just have leaves without any blooms, feed it with a very dilute feed (a seaweed base is often effective) once a week -"Weakly, weekly," as my grandmother used to say!—and put it outside at night. The combination of a tonic and a nightly temperature drop should bring on new blooms.

Plant an **instant feature**. If you're looking for an easy way to make an impact on your patio or terrace, plant an architectural plant such as a palm or a clipped topiary, phormiums or cordylines. These are perfect for pots: all they will require is regular watering and an occasional feeding. A truly spectacular example is the hardy banana *Musa Basjoo*, which grows 10 to14 feet high, several feet across, and produces glossy green leaves up to 6 feet long. One such plant could satisfy practically all your gardening requirements in itself!

Always take **cuttings**: you'll get more plants at no cost to pot up for gifts or to exchange with neighbors or fellow garden clubbers. To take cuttings from plants such as pinks and carnations, select non-flowering side shoots.

Prune early summer flowering shrubs as soon as their flowers fade to promote more flowers.

Beautiful foliage is the secret of a great garden because it looks good year round and lasts much longer than most flowers. Add texture with trees, shrubs and grasses as well.

You would be hard-pressed to find a foliage plant with such a variety of leaf shapes, sizes and colors as the Hosta family. Perfect for brightening up dull, shady spots next to north-facing walls or under trees, hostas thrive in borders as well as in pots. They are remarkably tolerant and will put up with short periods of drought or flooding, although moist but well-drained soil suits them best. Hostas come under a wealth of intriguing names, such as 'Elvis Lives' and 'Fried Green Tomatoes.'

Melianthus major provides not only **fantastic foliage** but flowers after its second year. Prune it in cold weather, and this plant will give you years of delight. *Heuchera 'marmalade'* is easy to cultivate, and it produces marmalade and green colored ruffled leaves and creamy flowers. It likes full sun to partial shade, grows up to 10 inches tall by 18 inches across and attracts hummingbirds.

Sea hollies provide wonderful texture. For great foliage contrast try them with *Actaea (cinnicifuga) simplex Atropurpurea* group, *Francoa ramose 'Rogersons Form'* or *Thalictrum decorum*.

Large plants can be split into smaller portions just like cuttings, providing you with more free plants. Use a spade and slice off sections from the plant's side or dig up the whole thing and cut or pull it into smaller pieces, each with its own shoots and roots. Replant the pieces right away and water thoroughly. Try this second technique with the slow-growing hellebore *(Helleborus multifidus subsp. Hercegovinus)* for example: a mature plant can be divided into well over a hundred finger-sized segments which can be grown in sun or light shade, in well-drained soil.

The metallic **blue oat grass** *Helictortrichon sempervirens,* which produces straw-colored flowers in the summer, makes a perfect foil for yellow flowers. It not only retains its good looks all year round, but it can spread to covers quite a large area.

Other ornamental grasses worth considering are zebra grass, *Chasmanthium latifolium, Miscanthus, Stipus* (ie. *Stipa tenuissima*) and molinia.

Don't put tulips in the same spot two years in a row unless you plant African marigolds where the tulips have flowered. The marigolds will restore the soil and you can then plant bulbs in the same spot again the next year.

English bluebells are invasive. This is great if you have a large empty patch and can't be bothered to do much with it, but it's not always desirable. The Spanish type, *Hyacinthoides hispanica*, is a less rampant variety.

Never plant **lilies and tulips** together because they suffer from the same diseases.

Pull away **tulip leaves** as soon as they become yellow and withered to prevent disease from entering the bulbs. Apply liquid fertilizer once a month or so to build the tulips up for next season. Use the money you save to buy new colors or varieties.

Try growing garlic close to plants susceptible to vine weevil, which is frequently found in new pots from even the best nurseries. Garlic is invasive, so keep it in a container or sink a pot in the ground.

If you want to produce outstanding **delphiniums**, remember that these plants need a steady amount of moisture at the roots during the growing season. Mulch will help keep moisture in.

Use thuja or taxus instead of leylandii as a **hedge** because it has the ability to grow new shoots out of old wood.

The secret of getting new ivy to cling to your walls is to cut it back hard after you plant it. New shoots get a grip right away, whereas old ones never do.

Cut off old stems as soon as their blooms have faded. This not only keeps your flower borders tidy, but it also saves the plants from wasting energy on producing seeds, which can result in the production of more flowers. However, it may be useful to allow plants like foxglove and columbine to go to seed. Allow the seeds will fall naturally, or collect them by hand to produce new plants and/or replace very old ones.

If you find you have an **excess of plants** don't just dig them up and throw them away, pot them into pots, wait until they've grown a little and give them to your friends as presents. Alternatively trade them at plant fairs or sell them at car boot or garage sales. Many charity shops will welcome them too.

Always check a plant's habits before you buy it. This is especially important for bedding plants. If you have a large garden and could do with lots of ground cover, violas, dwarf hyacinths, or anything that self-seeds is ideal. Some varieties of bamboo, for example are very invasive; others aren't. Some bamboo can grow ten feet in height during a week under the proper conditions. Make sure you get a plant that will do what you want it to.

Buy locally whenever possible. **Check state and national regulations before you bring any plants into your area. Imported plants can carry devastating diseases and pests or overrun indigenous flora.**

Medfly and kudzu are but two horrendous examples. Many, many individual people have had to pay hundreds of dollars or pounds to clear gardens of what looked like ivy or morning glory but was something else entirely! National and international consequences have been even worse, so please, **please** be warned and be careful.

How fair is a garden amid the trials and passions of existence.

Benjamin Disraeli

CHEAP LAZY LAWNS & LAWNMOWERS

For a **tough lawn** that will stand up to almost anything you and your kids dish out, sow grass seed with rye grass. The best sowing times are late March until May, or September through October, once there's some rain to encourage growth. Protect newly sown ground from the birds by stretching netting over it, and water lightly to settle the seed in.

Mow an **established lawn** at least once a week, but let the grass longer if the weather is hot and dry. Dig up weeds by hand before they get the chance to flower and spread their seeds. Aerate and top dress the turf seasonally.

Doing away with **benches, statues and island beds** in lawns saves finicky trimming around objects and speeds up the mowing process.

If you mow your lawn regularly, remove the catcher bag. **Fine grass clippings** won't build up into a thatch, and they will restore nitrogen levels and help protect the lawn from drought.

Choosing the **widest mower** you can afford reduces the number of times you have to walk up and down your lawn. Save time and energy for relaxing on it instead!

Keep lawns simple: the ideal shape is oval or softly curved and shows imperfections less than straight lines. Install lawn edging or put in a brick mowing edge so you won't have to trim the edges with shears.

To keep your lawnmower from **rusting**, wipe all the moving parts with a lightly oiled rag.

Check the condition of the blades regularly. Do they need sharpening, tightening or replacing? Preventative maintenance saves work and reduces repair costs.

Examine **electric mower cables** for any signs of wear or damage often. If you find even one, replace the cables immediately.

If you have a gas mower, drain the gas and **oil tanks** and clean the **spark plug** before you put the mower away for the winter. Fill the oil tank with clean oil but leave the fuel tank empty. Gasoline not only deteriorates over time, but it evaporates, and you don't want flammable vapors building up in your shed or garage.

Take care of mower repairs or part replacement in the fall. Don't leave this chore until spring: that's when all the other gardeners will be lining up to get their mowers fixed.

Never leave a power mower standing for months on a damp surface or in a damp place as it will inevitably be difficult to start in spring. Stand the mower on a piece of cardboard or a block of wood, and keep the area as well ventilated as possible to avoid condensation in the gas tank.

Spread the following recipe over your lawn each springtime to improve its general health and vigor. Mix together one 4 or 6 cubic foot bale of peat moss, two pounds of grass seed, two pounds of finely ground-up charcoal, two 30 litre bags of compost and half a pound of nitrogen. This amount should cover about a thousand square feet.

Water your lawn early in the morning, preferably when ground is dry, and really let the water soak in. To ensure a low-maintenance lawn, do not overwater!

Feed the lawn once in the spring and again in the late fall, using slow-release fertilizers to keep the grass growing evenly.

Set your lawnmower to its highest setting to keep the grass at least two inches high. Your lawn will not only look better and be healthier, but you'll have less work to do because the taller grass will shade out the weeds.

Avoid walking on your lawn when it's frost covered or waterlogged as compaction leads to root damage: the grass may be damaged or killed.

Leaves left on the grass may kill it, so rake them up and add them to your compost heap for free fertilizer next year.

The oldest and safest **weed kill**er is lawn sand. This can be bought ready made or easily mixed as follows: 3 parts by weight sulphate of ammonia to 1 part sulphate of iron and 20 parts fine silver sand. For maximum benefit distribute the mixture at the rate of 4 ounces per square yard when there is no chance of heavy rain for at least 24 hours.

If your lawn is looking patchy and worn and you want an easy fix, buy pre-germinated grass seed. A half pound (250g) pack will cover roughly 21 by 6 feet (7 by 2 metres).

Be safte around your Lawnmower:
Fill gas-powered mowers outdoors and keep cigarettes or other heat sources far away! Wipe up any spills and replace and secure the fuel cap immediately.

Do not turn a gas mower on its side to inspect the underneath because gas and/or oil will probably leak out.

Don't buy an electric mower that doesn't have a circuit breaker. This will prevent any nasty accidents if the mower comes into contact with moisture or the cable is damaged in any way.

Clear the lawn of any foreign bodies before you mow (and we don't mean the sunbathing au pair). Stray rocks, dog bones and children's toys can cause nasty accidents if they're picked up and spun out by the blades.

Never, never run the mower over gravel for the same reason.

Wear heavy shoes or boots when mowing if you want to keep all your toes, and save the loose clothing and dangly jewelry for another occasion.

If your hair is long, tie it back. This sounds obvious, but you'd be surprised at the number of people who have forgotten and later regretted it.

Mow across a slope rather then up and down. You will have better control over the mower and will be less likely to fall toward it.

Turn the engine off whenever you leave the mower unattended. Consequences may be similar to leaving baby in the bath while you answer the phone.

The truly lazy will be glad to learn that it is now possible to buy robot mowers. These cost well over £1000 ($1000), but once set up they can save you a huge amount of work. The more sophisticated models may be programmed to work automatically at various times and under various conditions.

If your **soil** is not up to par, apply an organic general fertilizer before seeding or laying sod.

If you are starting out with grass **seed**, divide it into two containers to promote even distribution. Scatter the contents of the first container, then sow the second. Be patient: it will probably take more than one season to establish a reasonable lawn.

Alternatively, consider **laying sod**. Order in advance for a good choice of the best quality available, and allow for a little more than you think you'll need. Soak it well once it's in, and if necessary top dress it with a sandy topsoil.

Get rid persistent lawn weeds such as plantains and dandelions easily under the right conditions. Just wait for dry, mild weather to pull the weeds and you'll save yourself considerable work and aggravation.

When a man sits down in front of a garden, or strolls around in it, he steeps himself in delight. Because the garden is a paradise.

Masaaki Noda

CHEAP LAZY COMPOSTS

A compost heap is probably one of the gardener's best friends, and it's also great for the environment. Compost helps you develop **healthier soil, hardier plants** and more **abundant organic vegetables**—and if you produce it yourself, it's free. By recycling part of your household waste you'll also reduce the amount of garbage being thrown into landfill sites, which in turn reduces pollution.

Start your compost heap with a composter provided cheaply by your municipality or build one yourself from scavenged boards. Then start your heap. For **best compost results**, make the first layer of twigs or cut branches for aeration. Old potato peelings, banana skins, the outer leaves of cabbage, fruit peelings, egg shells, tea bags and coffee grounds can all be added as well as dead leaves, lawn clippings and garden waste but always spread the mixture out to the edges of the container and tamp it down gently. Every now and again give the pile a quick stir to keep it aerated. When it dries out, sprinkle some water on it. If it is too damp, add some old paper towels, toilet paper cores or empty egg boxes—cardboard, not styrofoam. Depending on the texture of your compost you can use it in about 6 weeks, but for a better consistency wait a little longer, preferably two or three months. As the pile compacts, the bottom layer will mature more quickly. Use this and leave the rest to mature and keep adding to it. (Keep your compost heap small, or construct one with removeable board sides to get at the bottom layer). Rather than leaving your compost heap exposed to the elements, cover over the top with a tarp to keep nutrients from leaching through into the ground and to help keep heat in. After several months you should have a good compost mix to spread on your garden and you haven't spent a penny.

Comfrey (contains nitrogen, phosphate and potassium) and **nettles** (rich in nitrogen and iron) are excellent compost activators: their high nitrogen content helps the microbes to get working. Adding a little wood ash between layers also benefits the mix.

To make a great **organic liquid** feed for beans, tomatoes and other greenhouse plants, soak nettles and comfrey in water for a few weeks and strain off the liquid.

For compact, rapid, and easy composting use a **wormery**. Simple-to-use, inexpensive kits that come with full instructions are widely available both from garden centers and by mail order.

Flowers are angels rooted in soil.

Alexander Stoddard

CHEAP LAZY CLASSIC COTTAGE GARDEN CHOICES

The so-called cottage garden has the reputation of being **beautiful, informal, and relaxing**: it's the one that appears to have sprung up spontaneously. Bird houses, feeders and baths as well as picnic tables and picket fences add to the overall effect. The plants found in a cottage garden are generally inexpensive and not difficult to grow.

There is **no rigid design plan** in a cottage garden. Scatter a few packets of the recommended seeds closely together. Once the plants have started to grow and you can see what they look like, you can move them to wherever you think they look best. The perennials come back year after year, and some annuals will re-seed.

These are some of the **flowers we find do well in a typical cottage garden:**

Ceratostigma willmotianum	Forget-me-nots, Love in the Mist
Ceanothus	
Bluebells	Heather
Phlox	White lupins
Japanese anemone	Asters
Pratia	Dianthus
Rock roses	Night-scented stock
Cosmos	Pansies
Thrift	Snapdragons
Hollyhocks	Wallflowers
Delphiniums	Foxgloves
Hydrangeas	Dahlia
Chrysanthemums	Sedum
Rhododendrons	Peonies
Roses	Narcissus
Snowdrops	Daffodils
Crocus	Tulips
Geraniums	

Popular **herbs** include varieties of mint, dill, sage, parsley, basil, French tarragon, thyme, chamomile, rosemary and lavender. Fresh or dried, they can be used for cooking. Dried chamomile and mints also make soothing teas, and lavender is popular for sachets and potpourris.

Dahlias are ideal in a cottage garden and come in a huge range of varieties and colors. Pinch them back to avoid their becoming spindly.

Another cottage garden favourite, hydrangeas, can be cut in the fall, taken indoors and dried to make wonderful, long-lasting flower arrangements. They can also be sprayed silver, gold, or whatever color you like for the holiday season.

Confronted with the vision of a beautiful garden, we see something beautiful about ourselves.

Jeff Cox

CHEAP LAZY ANIMAL MAGIC

Make sure you know the toxicity of anything you take home or put in the ground since **some plants are poisonous to people and/or pets.** Children often like the look of berries and flowers and think they'd be tasty. In fact, it would be a good idea to check what's growing in your garden right now. Yes, we have mentioned this several times. It's **extremely important.** Plants and herbs are very potent: take extra care.

Protect your favorite flowers and vegetables from **rabbits, mice, rats and foxes** with a liberal mulch of prickly leaves such as holly, gorse or pyracantha. Planting these bushes all around your property will discourage burglars too!

Neighborhood **cats making you suffer?** Bury several small bottles up to their necks and filling them with a few spoonfuls of noxious-smelling ammonia will make them stay clear.

On still, sultry days lightly spray the surface of **fish ponds** with your hose to oxygenate the water and ensure your fish are happy and healthy. Also add daphnia and cyclops water fleas (available from aquatic centres) to new ponds to devour pea-soup algae, which can build up before your oxygenating plants are large enough to check it.

Rubbing alcohol (surgical spirit) is supposed to be a good deterrent against **cats**. Sprinkle a dilute solution around their preferred toilet areas in your garden. This one has the sanction of the Cats' Protection League too.

To encourage visiting **frogs**, which eat slugs, put some of your containers close to each other and water them frequently to create a cool, damp hangout. Put one or two frogs in the cucumber frame, they will live there quite happily in the summer enjoying the conditions and keeping flies at bay.

Hedgehogs are also great slug eaters. To invite hedgehogs into your garden, make them a home out of a plywood box about 14 inches by 12 inches by 16 inches. Drill ventilation holes, add a waterproof top and cosy bedding from straw or dead leaves, and leave/construct a narrow tunnel entrance about 14 inches long by about 6-inch diameter. Hide the box in an out-of-the-way corner or under grass and leaf debris.

If your **dog** is leaving bothersome yellow stains on the lawn, try adding some tomato ketchup to his or her feed. Whatever the secret ingredient is will bring an end to the patchwork effect.

Hanging reflective bird scarers such as aluminum pie plates, strips of foil or old CD's from trees and bushes is a cheap (cheep?) way to to keep the birds from eating your soft fruits. Netting is the best deterrent, however.

Winding small lengths of hose between plants helps keep cats and birds away: they don't like snakes and shouldn't come too close.

If you have a problem with **moles** in the lawn or garden, find the tunnels and place a small piece of gorse or holly in the bottom of each one. Some people have also found this effective for gophers. The prickly plant will keep the animals from returning. You can also poke a couple of the large (circa. 1 foot in diameter) wooden-staked windmills now found at craft and garden stores into the ground above the tunnels: the vibrations that develop when they spin deter the moles. Children running around on the lawn also create vibrations, keeping moles far away!

Citrus fruit peels, chilli pepper powder and eucalyptus oil should all deter **cats** from wandering into your garden. If the local cats like a particular area in the garden, say the salad bed or herb garden, place a high trellis around it: don't set it in too well because a bit of wobble will deter them even more.

Short spiky sticks placed throughout the garden will also discourage **cats**. Just make certain they're not placed where people might trip over them.

If, however, you want a space in your garden for your cat and others, provide an area for them by turning over some dirt in a place where you won't want a garden bed. Then get some pheromone spray from a vet or pet shop and spray that around the new area to **encourage feline visitors.** Planting catnip will also create abundant happiness for your furry friends!

Spreading alum around an area is also said to work against **rabbits** and **horses.**

To make your own **rabbit repellent**, mix 2 tablespoons of Tabasco sauce with a gallon of water and spray it on your plants. Otherwise try commercially available Repel or Millers Hot Sauce Animal Repellent. If you think you eat like a bird, consider that many birds eat twice their weight or more in a day!

To attract birds, put up nest boxes and feeders. Generally they like cereal grains and grass seeds. Also leave wild areas in the garden to provide natural seed and berry sources for them. Butterflies and ladybirds will also benefit, among other desirable insects.

Consider putting up bat boxes, and creating attractive habitats for other endangered species too.

Be like the flower, turn your face to the sun.

Kahlil Gibran

CHEAP LAZY
PEST & WEED CONTROL

Plant **crocus bulbs** close to lavender bushes and you'll find this protects them from **birds** which won't touch the bulbs.

Sink small plastic cups into the ground close to any plants that are being attacked by **slugs** and fill the cups with cheap beer. Guinness or real ale is best. In the morning simply tip the contents of the cup into the compost heap. Slugs love beer so much that they'll quite happily drown in it. What a way to go!

To keep **slugs and snails** away from vulnerable plants, crush some eggshells and place a good amount around the base of the plants: ash, grit and coarse sand are also supposed to be effective. Make sure they cover a wide area as these pests can stretch much farther than you might imagine.

Slugs and **snails** cannot abide copper, so wrap leftover copper wire or an unravelled copper-coated pan scourer around the base of a plant or the rim of a pot to keep them at bay.

To keep **slugs** and **snails** from getting into potted plants, smear Vaseline around the rim of the container.

Keep **green and black flies** and aphids off roses by planting garlic and chives next to your bushes. Once again, make sure the garlic is placed in a container and sunk into the ground because it can spread and be quite invasive.

To combat an attack of **aphids**, add a couple of drops of dishwashing liquid to a bottleful of water and spray it on your roses or whatever.
Aphids hate nicotine. A potent spray can be made for free from old cigarette butts. Drop approximately 40 to 50 butts **into a 2-liter plastic bottle** filled with water and leave the concoction alone for about two weeks. Pour **the liquid** off into a spray bottle and spray any aphid-ridden plants **well**.

If you're still plagued by aphids, finely chop some hot peppers, garlic or onions and soak them in a pint of water overnight. **Strain the solids** and spray the juice **onto the bugs**. This **method** works great on most plants, including flowers.

Calendula and poppies attract hoverflies, whose larvae eat **greenfly** and **other aphids**.

Plant basil and marigolds among tomatoes to prevent **whitefly.**
It's not that the whitefly particularly don't like these marigolds, it's because the pungent smell from the marigolds masks the nice smell of the tomatoes that usually attract whitefly.

Nettle spray is great as a general **insect repellent,** and **it's also high** in nitrogen. Fill a bucket with about 1/2 pound fresh young nettles and water, cover it and leave **the mixture** to ferment for a couple of weeks or so. Strain it and spray your plants. If you don't have any **nettles** growing in your garden try local parks, woods and roadside hedgerows. Add the remaining mushy nettles to the compost heap as it is a great activator.

Plant elder and mint to discourage **caterpillars,** and majoram and mint to help repel **ants.**

When pruning prickly shrubs like berberis and holly, save the **cuttings** and **let them** dry **out. Later,** when you come to sow your peas and beans, place the prunings in the **furrows** to keep away **mice.** This is a far safer method than the one used by Victorian gardeners, who used to roll seeds in red lead and paraffin to keep the rodents away.

Mice and **birds** can wreak havoc in a newly sown seedbed, but all will be well if you moisten the seeds with paraffin before sowing.

If your houseplants **are** suffering from an attack of dreaded **whitefly,** then try this novel remedy: suck up the majority of the whitefly with a vacuum cleaner, then stand the pot on a mirror. **Any** remaining whiteflies **will** become disorientated and fly away. This really works!

It's easy to prepare **elder spray,** which kills **aphids and small caterpillars** and is useful as a fungicide for **mildew** and **black spot** on roses. Make sure you use an old saucepan because **the toxic agent** you're releasing is **hydro-cyanic acid, which is poisonous. Be sure to label the pan so you don't use it for food preparation again.**

Gather a pound of elder leaves and young stems, preferably in spring when the sap is rising. Place the leaves and stems in the saucepan and add 6 pints of water. Boil the mixture for half an hour, adding more water as necessary, then strain it into bottles through old pantyhose lining a funnel. The mixture will keep for three months if bottled tightly while still hot. Use the liquid cold and undiluted.

Rhubarb spray. The oxalic acid in rhubarb leaves is a safe control agent for **aphids**, particularly those on roses. To make a rhubarb spray, cut one pound of rhubarb leaves, place them in a quart of water in an old saucepan (the oxalic acid may damage one that you still use) and boil the mixture for half an hour, adding water as necessary. Once it's cooled down add 1 dessertspoon of soap flakes dissolved in a cup of warm water. Stir the mixture thoroughly and use undiluted as a spray. If you don't have any rhubarb in your garden, ask a friend or neighbor or check with your grocer.

Applying a teaspoonful of salt to an individual lawn weed such as a **dandelion** can kill it.

Red spider mites love dry conditions and hate cold water. If you have an infested plant, mist it once or twice a day with a spray bottle you've kept in the fridge. The mites will soon find somewhere else to live.

Woodlice are a sign that your soil is healthy. They are very sensitive to pesticides and feed on organic matter that is abundant in natural production systems, so the more woodlice you have, the more wildlife-friendly your gardening methods. Look upon this as a compliment, even if they're not the prettiest creatures to have around.

Encourage birds to come into your garden by hanging **suet balls** or seed feeders and providing a birdbath or shallow fountain. Different birds eat different insect pests.

Grow primrose, marigolds, wallflowers and nasturtiums which attract beneficial insects like ladybugs, lacewings and hoverflies.
To get rid of **root aphids**, water with a dilute mixture of essential lavender or peppermint oil.

Dig out any identifiable **weeds** immediately, carefully removing all the roots you can find. Hoe any areas of bare soil (to a depth of no more than half an inch) on sunny days to keep weed seedlings from taking hold. Weeds may be tossed in the trash or left on the soil surface to dry out, then disposed of.

Spread a layer of compost or bark over the soil as a mulch to prevent weeds from sprouting. Old carpeting is also brilliant and very cheap or free.

Blobs of frothy white liquid known as **cuckoo spit** sometimes appear on plant stems in early summer, and the affected shoot tips may become distorted. This has nothing to do with cuckoos or any other bird; in fact, the condition is caused by an insect called the froghopper. Cuckoo spit is only a temporary problem, and it rarely causes much damage. You can blast it off with a strong jet of water or wipe it off with gloved hands.

Put a used teabag (any type) over the hole in the pot when you transplant. This not only allows water to drain out but also keeps **insects** out as well.

Keep your cabbages, broccoli and other green, leafy veggies safe from **caterpillars**, spreading newly mown grass clippings around their stems.

A strip of aluminium foil wrapped around the stems of young cabbage plants will keep **cabbage-fly larvae** from attacking them.

Use your vacuum cleaner to remove **flying insects and/or eggs** from your greenhouse. It's environmentally friendly, and there's no cost involved. Just remember to throw the vacuum bag into the trash immediately.

As the old gardener's saying goes, "One year's seeds, **seven years' weeds.**" In other words, you are inviting trouble if you leave weeds to flower and shed their seeds all around your garden: grab them when they first appear.

Snails are usually considered pests, however Miriam Rothschild tells of a cat called Nirvana who shared her lunch of chopped liver every day with a large Roman snail, which lived amongst the pansies in Elena Malagodi's roof garden. She does not relate if the method of domesticating snails was ever known to have a wider, practical, application for the average garden.

The average garden snail has a top speed of 0.03 mph.

The vine weevil, is a destructive beast even though it does not fly. Its grubs, which are white and look remarkably like fat maggots, may suddenly seem to be everywhere. If you find them in one pot, it is a safe bet they will be in most or all of the others, destroying anything they can get their chompers into.

If one of your potted plants has been doing well over the past few years but is suddenly not growing or looks decidedly unhealthy, check around its roots. If you see grubs, you'll have to take action immediately and remove them. Surgical gloves are handy for this. Sometimes drastic action is necessary and you may have to throwing the entire contents of the pot away. Warning: do not put it in with the compost! Bag it up separately and put it in the trash can.

Remember that vine weevils have to crawl up your pots before they can lay their eggs. There are various products on the market that you can paint onto the pots or containers to help prevent future infestations. It's always a good idea to check the compost for grubs before you repot.

Finally, don't panic every time you see an insect. Some creepy crawlies will be your best garden friends. That **spider** will eat almost all of the pest mentioned above, particularly juicy flies, so don't kill her. **A ladybird** will consume a huge number of aphids in one sitting. And the dragonfly zipping around your pond or water feature is a useful bug eater as well as a beautiful one.

What is a weed? A plant whose virtues have not yet been discovered.

Ralph Waldo Emerson

CHEAP LAZY POTS AND CONTAINERS

Recycle, recycle and recycle. All those **yogurt cups, soda bottles, cardboard cartons and tin cans** are the cheap lazy gardeners' delight. Start large seeds in egg cartons, small ones in styrofoam meat trays, avocado pits in soup cans and almost anything in the clear plastic containers your takeout salad or sandwich come in—just cut a drainage hole or two, and you've got an instant greenhouse!

To make a self **watering pot**, take any plastic **water or soda** container and cut it roughly in half. Take the cap off and punch a few holes around the mouth of the bottle. Reverse the top and slide it into the bottom portion (there will be a gap between the two sections). Fill the reservoir at the bottom and plant whatever you like in the top half. Add water to the reservoir as necessary. For a contemporary look cover each piece with aluminium foil, or leave your pot plain so you can see what plants look like underground.

Experiment with **larger containers**. Restaurants and caterers almost always purchase food wholesale, and you can often get jumbo-sized cans, tubs and jars for free once they are empty. The only limit on their use is your imagination, so think outside the garden too.

Old car tires make great **large planters**. Just stack up two, three or four and line with a plastic garbage bag. Put a layer of gravel in the bottom and add potting soil and the compost of your choice. Paint as desired: you can achieve some terrific effects. These home-made containers are ideal for small trees, shrubs and particularly potatoes if garden space is at a premium.

If you love **poppies**, why not grow some more for free? Once a plant has flowered, shake the seeds into a bag, label it and you'll be set to sow the following year. Poppy seeds are best germinated in pots under a garden frame. Sprinkled them onto an inch or so of gently **compressed potting soil** and cover with a very thin layer of about 1/8th inch of Perlite: if it's any deeper, the seedlings will exhaust themselves trying to reach the surface. Too much like work? Here's an alternate method of increasing the poppy population. Once the plants have gone to seed, work sharp sand into the soil around them and rake the seeds into it - you'll have a forest of youngsters next year in a great swathe of color to raise your spirits.

To **reduce water loss** and protect against frost, line the sides of your **outdoor** containers with bubble plastic.

Plants in pots need to be kept watered and fed. Never allow them to dry out, and feed them regularly during the spring and summer. Use a granular fertilizer top dressing in the spring and mix a liquid plant food into their water (see the label for dilution instructions) each week during the rest of the growing season.

Old wine barrels and tea chests make great planters for a variety of shrubs, flowering plants and even small trees. Use them to vary the levels of your plantings in a small area or to break up larger areas to advantage.

All kinds of plants may be grown in containers and moved around to create different combinations at will. Bedding plants are commonly grown this way, but it's worth try shrubs, herbs, alpines, bulbs, roses, herbaceous perennials, climbers, heathers, strawberries, dwarf fruit trees and conifers as well.

Herbs comfortable in containers include bay, curry plant, mint, pennyroyal, catmint, cotton lavender, marjoram, lavender, parsley, sage, rosemary, thyme, santolina, southernwood, woodruff, savory and alpine strawberry.

Hanging Baskets, which are always popular, are an immediate and relatively inexpensive way of brightening and softening dreary areas or bleak corners. They **may be hung or wall mounted: just be certain to use the proper hardware for the weight of the basket** *after the plant has been watered,* **and secure the bracket into a stud, preferably along the center.** Putting the basket onto a pulley mechanism will make maintenance much easier.

This is the basic planting method for hanging baskets.
Water your chosen plants well to start with, and if you don't have access to a suitable table or countertop, use a bucket to support your basket while you work on it. Use a piece of plastic or sphagnum moss to line the basket (if you're using moss, place a saucer at the bottom to help keep in the moisture). Fill the basket half way with a mix of potting soil, Swell Gell and slow-release fertilizer. Next take three flowering and three foliage plants to start with and plant them through the sides of the basket. Then fill the basket to the top with more potting soil mix and plant your tallest plant in the center. Take a further three flowering and three foliage plants and plant them around the edge of the basket, using more plants as needed for larger baskets. Then water the basket very thoroughly, until it's soaked through. Do this once again. Make sure the newly planted basket is protected both from frost and from strong sunshine for at least three days.

Remember to keep your hanging baskets and containers **well watered** and **well fed** (use liquid feed as the flowering season comes to an end and deadhead the flowers to keep them coming.

Here's a short list of plants that do well in hanging baskets:
- **Flowering:** begonia, felicia, geranium, mimulus, petunia, brachycome, fuschia, impatiens, lobelia, nasturtium, portulaca and nemesia.

- **Foliage:** nepeta, helichsrum, cineraria, lamium, plectranthus, lysimachia, Swedish ivy, creeping Charlie (any ivies, really) and my favorite, the unkillable pothos.

- **Herbs:** catmint, marjoram, lavender, apple mint, pennyroyal, creeping savory, alpine strawberry, and thyme.

Where flowers bloom so does hope.

Lady Bird Johnson

CHEAP LAZY CACTI AND SUCCULENTS

Cacti and Succulents have evolved all over the world to live in areas of low rainfall. They also produce some quite stunning flowers, some flower as much as a foot across. These particular plants know how to **store water** efficiently. There are about 7,000 to 9,000 different varieties with South Africa being the hot spot, it more ways than one. So for obvious reasons these plants are very good if you live in a particularly dry or sunny area as they tolerate drought very well.

Note that some of these have extremely **sharp pointed spikes** and these are dangerous for young children and for adults too - so double check for safety.

Aloe vera is a succulent used for many **medicinal purposes** and comes in many varieties and shapes and sizes.

The **Christmas & Easter** cacti produce exotic flowers during the dark part of the year. These will flower if you reduce the amount of daylight they absorb.

Ice plant *Sedum spectabile* is an easy choice; also agaves, aloes, aeoniums, fendleri, bonkerae, echinus, texensis and sempervivums.

Some **favorites** include *Echinopsis bruchii* which forms clumps and produces bright flowers, *Aeonium 'plumb purdy'*, the large *Agave colimana* and much smaller *Agave potatorum* with short toothy leaves, *Agave guiengola igal*, *Agave iguana*, *Aloe glauca* - easy, frost resistant with a bright orange flower, the tall *Aloe lutescens* and *Aloe potrerana*.

Shorter aloes are the *Aloe ukambensis* with a pretty dark red flower, the *Aloe schelpei*, *Aoe acutissima var. acutissima* and several *Aloe veras*.

The golden barrel cactus *(Echinocactus grusonii)* produces up to two foot clumps.

Keep dormant cacti dry during the winter to prevent basal rotting. Let cacti and succulents dry out completely between waterings. Water frequently in the spring and summer to encourage flowering. Repot cacti in late winter, but only if they are obviously too big for their pots.

If you see any bugs, which can hide in the furry like patches at the base of the plant, dab methylated spirits or rubbing alcohol on them.

Psychoactive cactii include the Donana, San Pedro, Peyotillo, Tsuwiri, Sunami, Dolichothele and *Lophophora Williamsii*.

Correct handling of flowers refines the personality.

Bokuyo Takeda

CHEAP LAZY LOW MAINTENANCE
HARDY PLANTS & TREES

Plants that thrive on neglect, that flourish in the poorest soil with only first season watering if that - these are the cheap, lazy gardener's best friends. Included are euphorbias, lavenders, artemesia, ceanothis, evening primrose, rosemary, phlomis and sages as well as the succulents above. Thrift or sea pinks, *Armeria maritime, Helianthum 'Wisley Primrose', Viburnum opulus, Euphorbia myrsinites, Geranium palmatum, Centranthus ruber, Eryngium x oliverianum, Hippophae rhamnoides, Stachys byzantina, Borzicactus aurespinus, Ulex europaeus and Phoriums* as well as the previously mentioned ornamental grasses make for a wide and varied palette.

Others to consider are the **smaller tulips,** which can be left in the ground all year, alliums, acanthus and the biennial horned poppy *Glaucium flavum* grow in the most uninviting places. Tiny cracks will provide the necessary foothold for the pink and white daisies of *Erigeron karvinskianus* which spreads abundantly, as well as thyme, helanthemum and cerastium.

Clematis viticella is probably the toughest clematis with masses of flowers, and the fragrant buddleia will attract butterflies galore. Both of these benefit from vigorous pruning after flowering. *Honeysuckle Belgica* features lovely looks and a gorgeous scent with a tough constitution.

For **larger plants, shrubs and trees** try the gooseberry ribes speciosum with its fuschia like red flowers, *Aloe porphyrostachyus, Furcraea longaeva, Dudleya, Hesperoyucca whipplei, Enogonum giganteum, Senna bicapsularis,* the Mexican *Palo verde, Aeonium arboeum, Tecoma stans,* Manzanita tree *Arctostaphylos Ruth Bancroft* and the *Eucalyptus erythrocorycap.*

Poppies are true friends to the cheap, lazy gardener. They come in a range of glorious, brilliant colours against decorative green foliage and bloom from May/June through the summer. Ranging from 12 in to about 4ft high, they flourish in sunny positions in well-drained loamy soil. They are easy to grow, need practically no care, self-sow readily, can be divided in the fall, and respond with gratitude to mulch in winter.

They look wonderful in swathes of the same color, or can be mixed or set against some other plants such as golden heliotrope, valeriana, artemesia, bronze fennel, delphiniums, phlox and asters.

There are myriad varieties of Poppies, some to start with include:

Allegro

Patty's Plum

Perry's White

Turkish Delight

Cedric Morris

Curlilocks

Picotee

Ferns are ideal denizens for shady woodland, sheltered and damp areas. They look wonderful in town gardens too, for example under rhododendrons or with hostas such as *Hosta sieboldiana*. Try hardy favorites *Belchnum chilense* which looks good all winter and the tree fern *Dickensonia Antarctica*.

Others include:
the versatile *Athyrium niponicum var. pictum* with splendid variegated fronds, the vigorous, upright emerald colored *Dryopteris felix-mas* and maidenhair fern *Adiantum pedatum*. By your pond plant the gorgeous purply shepherd's crook shaped *Osmunda regalis 'Purpurascens'* whose pale green fronds turn gold in autumn. Another visual delight is the majestic ostrich fern *Matteuccia struthiopteris*.

Dahlias are great mixed into sub-tropical style borders and marvellous for the patio - they look terrific and offer brilliant value for money. Dahlia tubers can be dug up in the fall, stored and replanted year after year - a top recycling star! Dormant tubers also can be "forced" to produce shoots for use as cuttings if tucked into small pots with a little compost. Once the shoots are about 2 in high cut them off at the base, pot into seed compost, water lightly and keep warm and humid until rooted. Nip the tiny tips to encourage branching out and feed lightly till well grown and ready to plant out, and presto! New plants for free.

Hellebores a wonderful choice of colors is now available. Hellebores are long lived and can last for decades in the garden and are well suited to light shade. They need space and fertile, deep ground to grow, their vast, copious root systems travelling far and wide searching for nutrients and minerals. Enrichment with spent mushroom compost or leaf mould will keep them flourishing and abundant. Cut off and burn old foliage to keep disease free from black spot fungus. Try *Hellebore orientalis* for flowers which start in late winter.

Snowdrops

Dormant snowdrop bulbs are prone to drying out. To avoid this and establish superb drifts of blooms in one swoop, plant growing bulbs in full leaf and flower.

Types to try include:

Galanthus augustus, Primrose Warburg, S. Arnott, South Hayes, Spindlestone Surprise, Cowhouse Green, Elwesii, Nivalis Flore Pleno.

Winter aconites are very easy plants and will reliably flower where almost nothing else will grow. It likes full morning sunshine, however it will also grown in woodland or shady spots that would rule out other plant life or in chalk, but good drainage is essential. The lovely yellow blossom will make a brilliant continuous carpet of bloom as the plant grows only to a height of about 4 inches and self seeds with vigor. It is easy to divide and transplant. This should be done whilst in full flower and leaf. Try *Eranthus hyemali*s and *Eranthus cilicus.*

Daffodils - "a drift of golden daffodils." Wordsworth's legendary flower adorning the hillsides now comes in an enormous variety of shapes and sizes. His original *Narcissus pseudonarcissus* at 10 inches high with simple warm yellow downturned flowers is but one of a crowd now including taller, bolder hybrids, often with double flowers as well as refined, graceful, diminutive models suitable for rock gardens. Easy to grow and versatile, daffodils are happy in soil conditions ranging all the way from open, warm and slightly alkaline, to tolerating semi-shade and neutral to acid ground. It does need to be well drained though.

Try *Narcissus cyclamineus* and *N. Bulbocodium* and *N. Soleil d'or* for grassy hillsides, *N. 'Baby Moon'* for scent and deep yellow flowers, *N. canaliculatus, N. 'Tete a tete'* and *N. Hawera* and *N. 'Jenny'* for rock gardens and pots, *N. 'Minnow'* and *N. 'Jumblie'* for wind-swept areas, *N. 'Sun Disc', N. 'Silver Chimes'* and *N. Thalia* for taller, later flowering varieties, and *N. 'Rip Van Winkle'* for a trouble-free easy going double flower which will flourish almost anywhere.

> None can have a healthy love for flowers unless he loves the wild ones.
>
> Fortes Watson

CHEAP LAZY TOP 50 FAVORITE PLANTS

Alchemilla mollis
(ladies mantle)   happy in shade and sun, a sight to please you
                               8 months of the year.

Astrantia major
(masterwort)   no effort to keep, blossoms for 5 months.

Erysimum Bowles Mauve
(shrubby wallflower)   create a "hedge" for eight months of delight.

Geranium macrorrhizum
'Album'
(Big root cranesbill)   plant en masse for the lowest possible
                               maintenance, fast spreading, fragrant leaves,
                               semi-evergreen.

Choisya ternata
(Mexican orange
blossom)   easy care, gorgeous scent and blossom.

Nandina domestica
(Heavenly bamboo)   just that!

Salvia patens   high impact color and no work.

Tropaeolum speziosum
(Scottish flame
thrower)   a great herbaceous climber.

Viburnum tinus
'Spring Bouquet'   terrific evergreen with flowers and berries
                               and no maintenance.

Cornusalba 'Elegantissima'
(Red twig dogwood)   beautiful coloured branches and superb   foliage.

Geranium x
cantabrigiense 'Biokovo'   spreads well, goes anywhere, dainty flowers.

Euonymous fortunei
'Emerald Gaity'
(Wintercreeper)   robust, longlasting, easy care.

Euphorbia amygladoides var. robbiae
(Mrs. Robb's bonnet) bright yellow flowers in spring, evergreen, dry soil, good in shade.

Hellborus x hybridus flowers from Jaunuary on.

Lonicera purpusii
(winterflowering honeysuckle) easy, easy and scent from November through March.

Hydrangea arboresens "Annabella" and

Hydrangea paniculata 'tardiva' two top choices!

Nepeta 'Dropmore'
(Catmint) long flowering, no maintenance, deer resistant.

Rubus pentalobus
(Crinkle-leaf creeper) ground cover all year round, weed suppressing, tolerates all sites.

Geranium 'Johnsons Blue' rich, sky-blue flowers, lovely deep green foliage, blooms June-Aug, drought tolerant, disease and deer resistant.

Viburnum plicatum 'Summer Snowflake' lovely flowers, autumn colour, no maintenance, excellent host to clematis.

Narcissus 'Jetfire' half normal size, yellow petals and orange trumpets, reproduces easily, plant and forget.

Abeliophyllum distichum
(White forsythia) fragile white/pink blossoms, heady almond scent, great for a sunny spot with well-drained soil.

Viburnum carlesii 'Aurora' fabulous scent, round clusters of flowers, attractive foliage, never needs pruning.

Primula 'Guinevere'	pink flowers with yellow centers, likes shade, easy, pretty and reliable.
Brunnera macrophylla 'Hadspen Cream'	blue forget-me-not flowers and large variegated leaves, easy to grow, slow to spread.
Rosa 'Jilly Cooper'	profusion of beautiful pale flowers with amazing scent - blooms through the summer.
Rosa 'Madame Gregoire Staechelin'	a climbing rose full of exuberance and huge joyful blowsy fragrant pink flowers for a warm, sheltered spot.
Snowdrop *Galanthus 'S. Arnott'* (Sam Arnott)	tall with large flowers, good for light shade with humus rich soil.
Lavendula x intermedia 'Grosso'	classic lavender with powerful scent. Clip after flowering, easy to grow.
Pelargonium 'Apple Blossom Rosebud'	rosy tipped cream flower clusters. Grow from cuttings replace yearly, no bother.
Verbena bonariensis	clusters of tiny mauve flowers float on long, wiry stems. Self-seeding biennial, which spreads anywhere happily.
Hamamelis x intermedia 'Pallida' (Witch Hazel)	slow growing tree, yellow foliage and pale yellow flowers pretty well all winter till March.
Rosa 'Magic Carpet' *Hellborus x hybridus*	lovely small pink rose, ideal ground cover. fantastic colors and evergreen foliage.
Syringa 'Sensation'	loads of purple outlined in white blossoms, good for heavy clay.

Cleodendrum tricholomum
var. fargesii — large shrub which erupts with late summer scented white flowers, star-shaped red calyces with turquoise berries in the fall.

Sedum telephium
'Matrona' — ideal for sun, dense pink flower heads on red stems, purply leaves, attracts bees and butterflies.

Lilium candidum
(Madonna Lily) — shallow planting in just alkaline soil, plant in autumn for tall lilies (3-6 ft) in June and July with up to 15 firm white blooms each.

Erithonium
hendersonii — a rockery plant which rabbits tend to avoid.

Aesculus pavia
(Red Buckeye Tree) — will grow to about 15 feet and produces red flowers in early summer.

Fuschia prosperity — a classic as to color and shape.

Aster novae-angliae
'Harrington's Pink' — disease-free New England aster.

Cotoneaster horizontalis
(herringbone
cotoneaster) — strong stemmed shrub with orange berries against small green leaves which turn red in the fall.

Dicentra spectabilis
(Bleeding Heart) — dark pink hearts with a white arrowhead centre: for cool, shady spots with rich soil.

Rodgersia 'Irish Bronze' — perfect pond side or bog perennial with wonderful foliage, creamy plumes of summer flowers, about 3 ft tall.

Tulipa 'Abu Hassan' — late spring bloomer with tall, strong stems and burnished copper colored petals changing to an orange rim.

Oriental Poppy *'Fruit Punch'*	early summer, red, orange and hot pinks, vigorous, free-flowering, virtually maintenance free, self-seeding.
Malus x robusta *'Red Sentinel'* (Crabapple)	great little fruit tree, small fruits last until March.
Chimonanthus praecox (wintersweet)	ideal shrub for a sunny, sheltered wall, spicy scent and translucent, bell-shaped yellow flowers.
Bizzi Lizzi	popular container flower - as long as you pick out dead heads regularly will produce a profusion of blooms all summer long.
Rosa 'Deep Secret'	easily grown bush with strongly scented large velvety dark red flowers from June till October.

If we could see the miracle of a single flower clearly, our whole life would change!

Hindu Prince Gautama Siddharta Buddha

58

CHEAP LAZY TOP TEN CLEMATIS

Clematis Asao-pink
Clematis campiflora
Clematis roogochi
Clematis Polis spirit
Clematis Huldane
Clematis recta purpurea
Clematis x diversifolia blue boy
Clematis Prince Charles
Clematis Pagoda
Clematis Olgae

CHEAP LAZY TOP FIVE CUT FLOWERS

Roses
Freesias
Sweet Peas
Lilies
Tulips

Find the seed at the bottom of your heart and bring forth a flower.

Shigenori Kameika

CHEAP LAZY TOP TEN EASY CARE TOUGH PLANTS

This list is comprised of the toughest plants around which need very little care to thrive.

Hedera helix 'Goldheart'
(Ivy)

a variegated ivy which likes the sun and well-drained soil: choose plain green for darker, colder walls. Self-clings to almost anything; rapid growth after first year.

Phormium cookianum 'Tricolor'

evergreen, sword shaped foliage, can grow to 6 ft high, ideal for sun and well-drained soil, unphased by pollution or wind, fine for the garden on beachside.

Crocosomia 'Lucifer'

prefers sun but flowers in the shade as well. Red flowers in summer; shiny, stripey foliage; frost hardy; grows to 3 ft; easy to divide in the fall.

Mahonia japonica

evergreen, scented sprays of yellow flowers from fall to spring, blue berries in May. Happy in shade, grows to 6ft.

Euphorbia polychrome

hardy perennial, grows anywhere to about 20 in. as to height and width. Lime-green blossoms spring or summer, self-propagates. Sap can irritate, so use gloves.

Lysimachia nummularia
(Creeping Jenny)

spreads anywhere, 2 in high, bright yellow flowers in summer. Good for rockeries and particularly good near a pond or water feature.

Clematis montana rubens

vigorous climber, reaching up to 30 ft, rapid growth, pale early spring flowers on old wood.

Alchemilla mollis	hardy, low-growing summer perennial thrives almost anywhere. Small summer sprays of lime-green flowers, which will self seed, grows to 20 in high and wide.
Hypericum ceratoides	evergreen, bright yellow flowers from May through summer, hardy and low growing almost anywhere, suppresses weeds, needs sun to flourish, grows to about 20 in high and wide, (check for immunity from rust).
Cotoneaster sp.	available in all shapes, sizes and varieties (deciduous, evergreen, semi-evergreen), good on dry soil, summer flowers and red or orange berries in fall.

When you have only two pennies left in the world, buy a loaf of bread with one, and lily with the other.

Chinese Proverb

CHEAP LAZY VEGETABLE GARDEN SNAPSHOT

Ideally look to **garden organically**, and consider raised beds for ease of access plus a fruit cage for soft fruit. Compost and manure are better for the soil and cheaper than chemicals, pesticides and commercial fertilizers. The hard work is in the initial soil preparation: once done this will save you a huge amount of weeding effort and also produce better results. Dig over the soil and break it up, removing all traces of weeds including roots and also large stones. About a spade's depth is usually sufficient. Then dig in some well-rotted manure or compost. Two spadefuls of compost or one of manure is ample for one square metre or about 10 square feet of soil. Don't overdo it or you will get soft, sappy growth and masses of pests. If you have really heavy clay, grow potatoes initially to improve the soil structure and save yourself a lot of effort!

In a reasonable sized patch grow:

(F1 = Hybrid)

Aubergine	Long Purple, De Barbentane, Thai Long Green
Beans	Sultana, Liberty Runner, Rob Roy
Broccoli	Claret F1, Tenderstem Green, Early White Sprouting
Beetroot	Boltardy
Brussels Sprouts	Maximus F1
Blueberries	Legacy, Herbert or Bluecrop
Courgettes	Eight Ball F1, Gold Rush
Carrots	Autumn King, Flyaway F1, Early Amsterdam Forcing
Chillis	Cayenne, Hungarian Hot Wax
Ruby Chard	Orange Fantasia, Fordhook Giant
Garlic	Purple Wight
Lettuces	All The Year Round, Cosmic, Lobjoits, Kendo Winter Density, Rouge d'Hiver, Robinson
Leeks	Musselburgh
Pumpkin	Oz, Rouge Vif d'Etampes, Baby Bear
Potato	Belle de Fontenay Desiree, Pink Fir Apple
Parsnips	Hollow Crown

Rocket	Apollo, Runway, Selvatica
Spinach	Hector F1, San Marco, Samish F1
Tomatoes	Ailsa Craig, Gardener's Delight, Sungold, Harbinger
Strawberries	Florence, Hapil, Mara de Bois, Elvira

In your vegetable garden include strawberries and apples as these lose considerable flavour in travelling. Home grown rocket, spinach, parsnips, tomatoes, radishes Tuscan kale and leeks are also a must for small spaces.

In pots try:

Aubergine	Diamond, Blue Devil
Chard	Bright Lights
Courgettes	Bambino F1
Chillies	Jalapeno
Kale	Vates, Flash
French Beans	Sultana, Kingston Gold
Globe Artichoke	Imperial Star, Emerald, Grand Beurre, Talipot
Garlic	Rossa di Saluggia
Lamb's Lettuce	Jade
Marrow	Cocozelle, Table Dainty
Potato	Charlotte, Pink Fir Apple
Radishes	Cherry Belle, Early Scarlet Globe, Icicle, Round white
Runner beans	Pickwick, Painted Lady Improved
Squash	Sunburst, Buttercup
Seakale	
Salad leaves	Mizuna, radicchio, red chicory, mibuna
Sweet Peppers	Gypsy, Sweet Banana, Lady Bell
Strawberrries	Elvira, Gariguette
Turnips	Purple Top Milan
Tomatoes	Tumbler, Red Pear Franchi, Garden Pearl

American Square Foot Gardening:
Ideally four square feet, so that you can rotate planting.
Try the following:

Beans	Cobra
Carrots	Early Amsterdam Forcing 3
Chevril	
Coriander	
Calabrese	Trixie
Garlic	Rossa di Saluggia
Lamb's lettuce	
Lettuce	Little Gem
Pea	Feltham First, Ne Plus Ultra, Asparagus
Potato	Charlotte
Pak Choi	Riko
Rocket	Runway, Apollo
Salad leaves	Mibuna, , mizuna
Shallots	Mikor
Spring Onions	Eiffel
Spinach	Lazio, Olympia, Tyee, Winter Bloomsdale
Tomatoes	Sungold, Brandywine

I'd rather love roses on my table than diamonds on my neck.
Emma Goldman

CHEAP LAZY TREE SNAPSHOT

Trees come in two main groups, deciduous and evergreen. Within these are different shapes and sizes, and those, which are especially good for foliage, flowers/fruit or color, and bark/berries. Here are some examples:

Deciduous
•Round/curvy shaped:

Gleditsia triacanthos 'Sunburst'	open canopy, yellow feather like leaves.
Prunus subhirtella 'Autumnalis Rosea'	lovely late flowering cherry.
Black Mulberry	spreading head of tangled branches, vine like leaves, delicious juicy fruit in fall.

• Column shaped:

Koelreuteria paniculata 'Fastigata'	delicate foliage, yellow in fall.
Prunus 'Amanogawa'	medium, narrow cherry with glorious flowers.
Aralia elata 'Variegata' Angelica	small black berries late summer.

• Open/airy:

Acer brilliantissum	Leaves open shrimp pink in the spring, turning gold in the fall.
Amelanchier lamarckii	springtime delicate, starry white flowers; black edible berries in fall and orange/red foliage.
Prunus serrula	Tibetan cherry with mahogany colored bark, white flowers and green leaves in spring, yellow leaves in fall with berry-like fruit.

• Weeping/drooping:

Morus alba 'Pendula'	weeping mulberry with glossy, heart-shaped leaves and mulberries in summer.
Pyrus salicfolia 'Pendula'	ornamental pear, creamy flowers in spring, silvery leaves, inedible fruit.
Betula youngii	weeping birch with classic colors.

Evergreen
- **Round/curvy shaped:**

Photinia x fraseri
'Red Robin'

glossy, brilliant red foliage plus small white flowers and spherical red fruits.

Cotoneaster Watereri
'John Waterer'

white flowers in summer and bright red berries in fall.

Arbutus unedo

red-brown bark sheds constantly, bright green glossy leaves, white, bell-shaped flowers and strawberry like fruit, prefers a sheltered spot.

- **Column shaped/long thin shaped:**

Juniperus scapulorum
'Skyrocket'

fantastic grey-green juniper.

Laurus nobilis

bay tree with aromatic leaves of dense, glossy green, yellow flowers in spring and black berries in fall.

Taxus baccata 'Fastigiata
Aureomarginata'

bright, fleshy red fruits in the fall on the female plants.

- **Open/airy:**

Olea europaea

olive with delicate grey-green foliage and small, fragrant white flowers in the summer.

Sophora microphylla

masses of open twigs with tiny olive-green leaflets: yellow pea-shaped pendulous flowers in winter and early spring and brown seed pods for year-round color.

Eucalyptus pauciflora
subsp. Niphophila

sheds silver white bark from summer to autumn making patterns beneath; grey-green leaves. Grows up to 80-100 feet.

- **Conical shaped:**

Cupressus arizonica var.
glabra 'Pyramidalis'

feathery, dense, blue-green foliage; compact and narrow and fast growing.

Brewers Spruce	distinctive deep green drooping curtain-like foliage; slender and upright.
Ilex aquifolium 'J.C. van Tol'	English holly with bright berries in winter and glossy dark green nearly prickle-free leaves.

Five Trees for Small Gardens:

Amelanchier lamarckii	starry white flowers, coppery leaves in spring, dramatic autumn leaves and winter-time purply-black berries.
Prunus x subhirtella 'Autumnalis'	(Winter-flowering cherry) - delicate pinky flowers from October to March, bronzish leaves turning gold in fall.
Acer griseum (Paper-bark Maple)	pretty leaves in spring, bonfire colours in the fall with delicate, peeling cinnamon colored bark. (Expensive but gorgeous!)
Crataesus monogyna (Hawthorn)	very hardy, white flowers in spring, berries in the fall.
Sorbus vilmorinil	fern-like leaves which turn red and purple in fall, white summer flowers followed by pearl-like pink berries.

Everyone has their favourites: ours are apple, cherry or plum blossom, Japanese maple, silver birch, holly, crab-apple, mountain ash, beech, oak, juniper, pine, cedar, hornbeam, yew, mulberry, willow, olive, almond, walnut, eucalyptus, chestnut, orange.

If seeds in the black earth can turn into such beautiful roses, what might not the heart of man become in its long journey towards the stars?

G.K. Chesterton

CHEAP LAZY HERBS & THEIR USES

Although most of us grow herbs for their culinary uses they can also be grown for pot-pourri, medicinal or ornamental purposes. If you have children and a small space in the garden encourage them to plant and look after the herb garden, they will also be more inclined to eat whatever they have grown expanding their food variety.

Herbs range from plants grown annually from seed, such as Basil, to more permanent perennials, such as Tarragon, and shrubs that include Rosemary, Lavender and Bay.

Herbs grown from seed should be sown in the Spring. Perennials, including Chives and Marjoram, should be planted in spring and summer. Shrubby herbs, Sage for example, can be planted all year round. If you're a lazy gardener go for the perennial varieties.

For best results plant herbs in a South or West facing border. This protects from cold and frost, and sunshine will light up the ornamental foliage of many varieties to wonderful effect. Good drainage, compost, feeding and watering will keep them healthy and vigorous.

Pruning
Herbs such as Cotton Lavender, The Curry plant, Garden Lavender, Rosemary and Sage benefit from a hard pruning in early to mid spring. Others such as Bay can be clipped into shape.

Feeding
With all plants where foliage is an attraction, an annual feed in the spring with a general fertiliser will give best results.

Herbs have so many uses it's hard to know where to start! Here are some suggestions:

Cooking
Basil, Chives, Dill, Hyssop, Mint, Rosemary, Tarragon, Chervil, Curry Plant, Germander, Marjoram, Lovage, Nasturtium, Savory, Thyme, Fennel, Coriander, Bay, Woodruff, Sorrel, Rocket.

Pot Pourri
Bergamot, Camomile flowers, Rosemary, Lemon Balm, Lavender, Sage, Catmint.

Drinks
Lemon Balm, Bay, Bergamot, Woodruff, Angelica, Alpine Strawberry.

Flower Arranging
Southernwood, Sweet Rocket, Rosemary, Angelica, Lavender, Fennel, Bergamot, Cotton Lavender.

Ground Cover
Catmint, Sage, Mint, Pennyroyal, Lemon Balm, Marjoram, Santolina, Cotton Lavender, Camomile.

Low Hedging
Rosemary, Lavender, Curry Plant, Santolina, Savory, Germander, Sage, Cotton Lavender, Southernwood.

Aromatic Leaves - Scented Flowers
Mint, Sage, Rosemary, Sweet Rocket, Cotton Lavender, Catmint, Savory, Curry Plant, Southernwood, Lavender, Marjoram.

Miscellaneous
Some uses for the following: Candied Angelica for cake decoration; Lavender in an oil burner or in the bath to aid relaxation. Camomile instead of grass as a lawn. Cotton Lavender to repel insects. Mint as a bath additive to help relax **(eau de cologne)**. Bay for topiary in the garden.

Herbal delights. The flowers of many herbs have a milder, sweeter taste than their leaves, so try adding basil flowers to a tomato salad, those of chives to egg dishes, thyme and hyssop flowers to chicken dishes, marjoram on pizzas and mint blooms to vinaigrette. Basil, chives, chicory and salad rocket flowers can be added to soured cream, yoghurt or crème fraiche to make an unusual dip or an accompaniment to baked potatoes.

Herbes De Provence Oil
This is great for salads or for brushing on to grilled fish
16cm (6in) sprig of rosemary
4 sprigs of thyme
12 basil leaves
4 bay leaves
3 split cloves of garlic
1 tsp of dried green peppercorns
2 slices of dried orange peel
2 dried flower heads of lavender
Extra virgin olive oil.

Place all the ingredients in a sterilised bottle and top up with the extra virgin olive oil. Store it for a month before using.

Parsley
Cultivated for thousands of years, used by the Greeks to crown victors and as feed for horses, and later in Ireland to keep fleas at bay. Now used as a garnish for many dishes, commonly either curly *(Petroselinum crispum)*, or flat leaved (French). As a companion plant will keep onion flies away and deter carrot flies, and grows well with tomatoes too. Needs good deep soil for its long tap root and regular watering and feeding. Keeps well in the freezer.

Lemon balm has been used for over 2,000 years through to the present day for everything from preventing baldness, curing toothache and as a love charm as well as strengthening memory, relieving headaches and chasing away melancholy. Apart from acting as a mild anti-depressant, drinking the tea after meals eases digestion and colic. An infusion of the leaves will help heal and prevent cold sores. Crushed leaves rubbed on the skin will repel insects and also reduce itchy insect bites.

Low fat yoghurt and **chives** make a healthier alternative to the traditional sour cream & chive recipe. Great on jacket potatoes and vegetables.

Mix plain low fat yoghurt with salt & pepper and a generous hand full of chopped chives and chill if preferred. For a dressing with extra bite add a glove of crushed garlic to the mix.

A generous sprinkling of **chives** in your mashed potato adds color and texture.

Dried herbs bought in your local supermarket can be expensive, what better way to add to your food to liven up dishes then to stroll into the garden and snip whatever quantity you like.

Herbs will **dry** very well in a container or brown paper bag in the salad crisper of the fridge, so you can enjoy your herbs all year round. Many often freeze well too.

For a **fresher alternative** you can put some in each ice cube compartment and add to your cooking whenever required.

Perfumes are the feelings of flower.
Heinrich Heine

CHEAP LAZY CHILDRENS' CHOICES

Check your garden for **toxic plants** and remove any before you allow children or pets to investigate. Children can't resist colorful berries or seeds and many poisonous plants are very pretty. Pets too are vulnerable so **double double check for** safety.

Ponds are great, but dangerous for children who have been known to drown in inches of water in but a moment. If your garden has one, fill it in and use it as a sand pit which the kids will love! (Make sure you have a lid for it to keep animals out).

Take your children to the park and see what sparks their interest. Then see what you can copy or apply at home for free or minimal cost. A used car tire on a rope makes an excellent **swing** if you have a good strong tree branch available to hang it from.

Sprout some **beans** on your windowsill with your children's help. When they are a reasonable size your children can pot them out in the garden in a special childrens' garden area. Having their own gardening gloves and rubber boots and tools will encourage them to have a try with a variety of plants.

Potatoes are also a great crop for children to experiment with. Seeing where chips come from is always an attraction! If you grow the potatoes in large pots you will get a cleaner crop than if you plant them in the ground. Use any strong, deep container of around 14-16 inches in diameter (36-40cm) which has good drainage holes. Early potatoes are a good choice.

Find a sheltered spot which gets the sun for your container. Put some broken crocks or some rocks in the bottom for drainage and then a layer of potting soil about 6 inches (15cm) deep. You then put three seed potatotoes with the sprouting side pointing up carefully on the soil and cover with another layer, this time around 4 inches deep (10cm). Water thoroughly.

As the shoots begin to come up, once they have reached 8 inches, top up with more potting soil, leaving the top halves of the shoots clear, and add some liquid feed when you water them. Keep topping up every two weeks or so. The potatoes will flower and be ready to harvest in about 10 weeks.

If you are planning a **patio**, get the kids to help out and have some fun by working out an area for them to **mosaic**. This will stretch their imagination and occupy them for ages, plus they will be able to show off the result for years to come. This can be used to create permanent squares for hopscotch or other games too.

Brighten up your garden with colored pots. Get the children to paint them or cover them with aluminium foil or plastic wrap. Have them paint their initials on their own individual pots and grow the plants of their choice in them.

Try a cheap ball attached to a pole by a rope for garden entertainment for kids.

Mobiles look great in the garden, and children love to make them. Try old CDs, beads, copper wire, old costume jewelry, wire coat hangers, old furniture handles, bits of chain, contents of your junk drawer... their imagination can be your garden's decoration!

Create a daffodil maze in the lawn with the kids, and/or a grass topped bench, and/or special bird trees with feeder platforms.

Make bird, bug, bat or bee houses with the children. They will get a great understanding of natural life cycles from making and siting these, and watching them being made use of.

Strawberries and cherry tomatoes can also be grown easily in buckets.

Find some old garden chairs at garage sales or thrift shops. Let the kids choose one each and paint or decorate them anyway they like. Give them a chance at the garden fence and the shed as well for some spectacular results!

If your children have art classes at school encourage them to make sculptures or ceramic pieces for the garden. Then have a picnic or a barbecue and ask over lots of their friends and yours for an exhibition.

To pick a flower is so much more satisfying than just observing it, or photographing it... So in later years, I have grown in my gardens as many flowers as possible for children to pick.

Ann Scott-James

CHEAP LAZY DISABLED EXTRA

For comprehensive information on gardening contact the marvellous UK charity **Thrive** at their national office: The Geoffrey Udall Centre, Beech Hill, Reading RG7 2AT, telephone 0118 988 5688, fax 0118 988 5677.

They work extensively on promoting well-being and social inclusion for all. Among their projects are the Thrive St. Mary's Garden in Hackney near the Geffrye Museum to help young offenders and HIV sufferers, the Battersea Garden Project in Battersea Park for those with learning disabilities, mental health problems, sensory or physical disabilities and rehabilitation and the Trunkwell Garden Project near Reading for young people with special educational needs.

In the US and Canada contact Easter Seals at: 230 West Monroe Street, Suite 1800, Chicago, Illinois 60606, USA tel. 312 551 7147, fax 312 726 1494 and 1185 Eglinton Avenue East, Suite 706, Toronto, Ontario M3C 3C6, Canada, tel. 416 421 8377, fax 416 696 1035, e-mail: info@easterseals.org.

Also City Farmer in Vancouver have a great handbook - contact City Farmer, #801, 318 Homer Street, Vancouver, B.C. V6B 2V3, Canada.

Plan your garden and what you are going to do when gardening before beginning to save yourself time and effort. Warm up before you start too, to get your circulation going and to loosen up the muscles and avoid strain.

Don't get overtired: rest every so often and have a hot or cold drink.

Keep your tools near you in a bucket or carrier, or on you in a gardener's apron to save trips back and forth to the tool shed.

Kneeler stools with padded knee rests and handles to help you get up are easily available.

Keep adjacent to a seat so that you can rest easily. Plan on weeding defined patches of your garden to complete in one session so as not to get carried away.

Check what soil conditions you have and choose plants to suit: much cheaper than losing the plants or trying to change the conditions.

How long will it take for your chosen plants to grow to maturity? How much maintenance do they need, and what sort? How much strength and/or interest do you have? Small, easy to handle plants may suit you best and be cheapest to buy and maintain.

Look for disease-resistant, thornless shrub roses which bloom for ages, slow growing dwarf conifers, low maintenance shrubs, climbers which don't need supports, self-seeding flowers, small vegetable patches and flower beds with wide footpaths for easy access, automatic irrigation systems to save water and carrying watering cans, herbs and fruit grown in easy access containers.

Is getting around the garden difficult for you? You may need wide paths and non-slippery surfaces. Wheelchairs need firm surfaces and fairly level ground. Are any steps easy to negotiate? Do you need handrails or resting spots? Are edges of paths and steps easy to see?

Walking frames, portable seats or electric buggies can make a big difference to your stamina and safety in the garden. Any with baskets attached will also be a great help.

Gardening tools with thick handles set at an angle for use without straining fingers or wrists are available from several suppliers such as ricability. Long handled rakes and forks reduce the need to bend. Many of these have snap on heads which makes them lighter and easier to carry about.

If you have arthritis or difficulty gripping, look for specialist tools made to make things easier. Super grip hoes, for example, can be obtained from www.peta-uk.com or www.gardenscape.ca.

A cheap way to help with uncomfortable handles of mowers, shear or other tools is to buy a pair of foam bicycle handle grips. Slip the grips over the tool handles, using washing up liquid or Vaseline to slide them on easily if necessary.

Ratchet pruners are much easier to use and make it possible to cut through a branch in just a couple of squeezes.

Wheelbarrows can be unstable and difficult to use: look for those with two wheels and easy grips which you can steer with one hand.

Exhibitions and garden shows can be great places to buy tools and get ideas on gardening. You can handle things on the spot and see if you like the feel of them, and large discounts are often available.

In buying or planning seating consider the materials in terms of weight, strength and maintenance, height, comfort of back and armrests, and proposed position. All of these will affect how much you use and enjoy it!

You can get Velcro plant ties which are much easier to use than string or wire.

Sink a drainage pipe about a foot deep next to recently planted trees to ensure that water goes directly to the roots. Save both effort and water!

Make sure your hoses have snap fittings for hose accessories, sprays and sprinklers to make life easier.

Plastic containers are lighter and cheaper than terracotta or ceramic and keep plants moist much longer. Make sure they have adequate drainage holes to avoid waterlogging problems.

Slow release fertilisers will save you a lot of work: they can provide nutrients throughout the season and on for up to 18 months on one application.

Choose dwarf fruit trees and grow them in containers for easy access. Potatoes, tomatoes and strawberries are also easily grown in pots or buckets. Gooseberries, raspberries and red currants are helped by an annual mulch and regular watering but otherwise don't need a much work and provide loads of fruit.

Raised beds can help make your gardening plots more accessible. To minimise maintenance consider the "no-dig" method of growing. Information on this and much more can be obtained from the Henry Doubleday Research Association at www.hdra.org.uk.

Brute force crushes many plants. Yet the plants rise again. The pyramids will not last a moment compared with the daisy.

D.H. Lawrence

CHEAP LAZY SPIRITS OF PLACE

Garden gnomes are the descendents of stele erected millennia ago to celebrate and promote fertility in the land, and by extension in people! Other "spirits of place" include fairies and leprechauns, trolls, devas, and angels (top quality help, all yours for just a "thank you").

Every culture since the dawn of time has emphasized working with nature and honouring the spirits of the earth itself, respecting the plants and flowers and trees, wildlife, and the air and water. Rituals grew up over time seeking guidance from the stars and cosmos as to the times to plant and reap, to work in harmony with nature so as to thrive and prosper, protected from harm.

Celebration of the seasons was seen as key, including the Spring, Summer, Autumn and Winter equinoxes, and working with the elements as in the oriental recognition of the importance of feng shui (wind and water).

A well-known and well documented modern example in the west of the power of working with angels or devas and the spirits of nature can be found at Findhorn in Scotland, where Peter Caddy and his community settled in 1962. They would have been hard put to have chosen a more unlikely spot, yet thrive they did. From their first season onwards their extraordinary garden flourished as they followed spiritual guidance.

According to Sir George Trevelyan, who subscribes to these beliefs as well as being a member of the Soil Association, there are four basic ways to invoke spiritual help in the garden. These are:

• Recognise and acknowledge the existence and presence of the spirits, communicating by offering them love and thanks.
• Ask for their help mentally or by speaking aloud.
• Be alert for their guidance in your thoughts or feelings or ideas.
• Take notice of any mistakes you make and don't repeat them.
• Give sincere thanks for receiving their help and for the positive results that flow from it.

Encourage birds: song and vibration are known to have healing effects and the chorus at dawn and dusk gives a boost to your garden.

All living things and the elements have a reason for being. Work in harmony with nature, and nature will reflect back what you put into it.

The archangel who looks after the planet is Uriel (the Fire of God), the archangel of the East, whose element is air.

Each direction, element, day, month, season and zodiac sign has an angel assigned to it. If you connect with the appropriate angel you are likely to get the best results in your garden. Note this can vary in the southern hemisphere as the seasons there differ.

North:	Michael	(Who is like God)
South:	Raphael	(The Healing of God)
East:	Uriel	(The Fire of God)
West:	Gabriel	(God is my Strength)

Monday:	Gabriel	Plant willow, vervain, birch, white iris
Tuesday:	Uriel	Plant rose, daisy, pine, pepper, thyme
Wednesday:	Raphael	Plant lavender, periwinkle, cherry, fern
Thursday:	Michael	Plant buttercup, oak, beech, cinnamon
Friday:	Uriel	Plant heather, sage, clematis, birch, ivy
Saturday:	Raphael	Plant coltsfoot, myrrh, fir, moss
Sunday:	Michael	Plant sunflower, cedar, heliotrope, marigold

	Northern Hemisphere	Southern Hemisphere
January:	Gabriel	Verchiel
February:	Barchiel	Hamaliel
March:	Machidiel	Uriel
April:	Asmodel	Barbiel
May:	Ambiel	Adnachiel
June:	Muriel	Hanael
July:	Verchiel	Gabriel
August:	Hamaliel	Barchiel
September:	Uriel	Machidiel
October:	Barbiel	Asmodel
November:	Adnachiel	Ambiel
December:	Hanael	Muriel

Spring:	Amatiel
Summer:	Tubiel
Autumn:	Tariel
Winter:	Amabiel
Wind:	Uriel, Moriel
Water:	Gabriel, Matriel, Ariel
Earth:	Michael
Fire:	Raphael
Aries:	Raphael
Taurus:	Michael
Gemini:	Uriel
Cancer:	Gabriel
Leo:	Raphael
Virgo:	Michael
Libra:	Uriel
Scorpio:	Gabriel
Saggitarius:	Raphael
Capricorn:	Michael
Aquarius:	Uriel
Pisces:	Gabriel

Don't try to force anything, let life be a deep let go. See (God/Spirit/All That Is) opening millions of flowers everyday without forcing the buds.

Bhagwan Shree Rayneesh

CHEAP LAZY LANGUAGE OF FLOWERS

Flowers have been used to decorate and underline special occasions of all types for millennia. The Greeks crowned their Olympic athletes with wreaths of parsley and laurel; Romans and Egyptians showered their rulers with flower petals and adorned their homes, celebrations and banquets with superb floral displays. In the East too flowers were brought to temples and sent to friends to intercede with the gods or as a mark of respect or thanks. May Day and Harvest festivals emerged from these ancient rituals and ceremonies.

In England the language of flowers became popular in the reign of Charles II but really came into its own with Lady Mary Wortley Montague as a clandestine method of receiving illicit love letters. The Victorians published any number of floral phrase books to assist deciphering bouquets. Here are some of the more commonly ascribed meanings:

Acorn	Immortality
Acacia	Secret love
Almond	Hope
Ambrosia	Love returned
Angelica	Inspiration
Arum Lily	Ardour
Balsam	Impatience
Bay Leaf	Strength
Bluebell	Humility; constancy
Cactus	Endurance; warmth
Calendula	Joy
Camilla	Admiration
Carnation	Bonds of affection
Chrysanthemum	Cheerfulness
Clover	Good Luck
Daffodil	Respect
Dahlia	Good taste
Daisy	Innocence
Dandelion	Wishes come true

Eucalyptus	Protection
Fern	Sincerity
Forget-me-not	True love
Forsythia	Anticipation
Gardenia	Secret love; you're lovely
Garlic	Courage; strength
Geranium	Preference
Hazel	Reconciliation
Heather	Good Luck
Holly	Defence; Goodwill & Happiness
Hyacinth	Loyalty
Iris	Faith
Ivy	Friendship, fidelity
Jasmine	Amiability, attracts wealth
Jonquil	Desire
Juniper	Protection
Kingcup	Desire for riches
Laurel	Ambition
Lavender	Devotion
Magnolia	Sweetness; beauty
Marigold	Comforts the heart
Marjoram	Joy and happiness
Mistletoe	Kiss me
Moss	Maternal love; charity
Myrtle	Love
Narcissus	Ego
Nasturtium	Conquest
Orange Blossom	Love
Orchid	Love; beauty; refinement
Palm	Victory; success
Pansy	Think of me
Parsley	Festivities
Peach	Longevity

Peony	Aphrodisiac
Petunia	Resentment; anger
Pine	Hope
Poppy	Pleasure; wealth
Primrose	Can't live without you
Queen Anne's Lace	Fantasy
Quince	Temptation
Rose	Love
Rosemary	Remembrance
Rue	Disdain
Sage	Long life
Salvia	I think of you
Shamrock	Light heartedness
Snowdrop	Hope
Spider flower	Elope with me
Spindle Tree	Your charms are engraved on my heart
Star of Bethlehem	Atonement
Stephanotis	Happiness in marriage
Stock	Lasting beauty
Strawberry	Perfect goodness
Sunflower	Loyalty
Sweet pea	Pleasure; departure; thanks
Syringia	Memory
Sweet Rocket	Deceit
Thrift	Sympathy
Thyme	Strength; courage
Tulip	True love
Valerian	An accommodating disposition
Violet	Modesty
Wallflower	Fidelity in adversity
Water lily	Purity of heart
Wisteria	I cling to you
Woodruff	Sweet humility
Wood Anemone	Frailty

Wormwood	Absence
Xeranthemum	Cheerfulness
Yarrow	Healing
Yew	Strength; sorrow
Zinnia	Thoughts of friends

Flowers have spoken to me more than I can tell in written words. They are the hieroglyphics of angels, loved by all men for the beauty of their character, though few can dechiper even fragments of their meaning.

Lydia M. Child

CHEAP LAZY LAST WORD (or so)

A pot pourri of cheap and lazy or just entertaining extras of all sorts!

For a relaxing, **low maintenance garden**, experiment with surfaces and dividers of different kinds such as various sizes and colors of gravel, brick, concrete, paving, stepping stones, decking, broken slate, railway sleepers, wooden packing crates, driftwood, tiles, wooden fencing, trellises, screens, hedging, bamboo, woven hurdles etc.

Pergolas create a focus in the garden, shade in summer and support for climbing plants of many types, as well as for a hammock or swing seat. They are fun to decorate and great to sit out in. They also add height and interest, not to mention shade if your grow climbers up them and needs no maintenance except a 5 yearly coating of wood preservative or a re-paint.

To make a small garden look larger or to add interest to a larger one, consider creating a **trompe l'oeil** (to deceive-the-eye) effect - cheap, easy and effective. This is usually a painted landscape or architectural detail, and with some plants in front can look brilliant. **Mirrors** can also be used to add depth and interest, or try other reflective surfaces for a different texture. If fixing a mirror anyway make sure it is fixed securely, do not 'free hang' a mirror or any decoration that can cut.

Add variety and experiment with different surfaces: sizes of gravel, brick, concrete, paving, stepping stones, decking. **Add color** by using different coloured gravels and slates.

The **pansy** is a symbol of love, hence its old name of Hearts ease. On no account must you pick a pansy with dew on it, as this will cause the death of a loved one. If pansies are picked on a fine day, this will ensure rainfalls. So remember this next time there's a drought.

Sloes are not only good for making sloe gin from the fruit. An infusion of the flowers can be used to treat diarrhoea, bladder and kidney disorders, weakness of the stomach and catarrh.

One of the **earliest** and welcomest of the spring flowers is the primrose. Needless to say it's steeped in folklore. It was believed that fairies used to shelter under the bloom and country people used to rub the leaves on their cheeks to produce a pleasing blush! Primrose tea was a good cure for worms and the leaves added to salads are supposed to help arthritis. Please don't pick the wild primrose, as it is a protected plant.

Remove **dead leaves**, which have fallen on heather plantings as if left they can kill the plant beneath.

Always buy strong, good quality **tools** and look after them well. If you can afford it buy stainless steel they will last a lifetime and are easier to clean.

An old **hot water bottle** filled sparingly with foam rubber chips (these can usually be found in packaging) is a handy **kneeling pad** for long jobs.

Did you know? An individual grey **field slug** has the potential to produce 90,000 grandchildren.

Brazil is thought to have the most native plant species; 56,000 estimated to date, and growing!

The most widely grown plant in the world is **wheat**. It has been cultivated for over 7000 years in every continent excepting only Antarctica.

Always spray **insecticides** in the **evening** to avoid the risk of harming bees, butterflies etc.

If you have **large spaces** in your garden which you would like to fill and have little money to cultivate plants, then fill up the space with a **garden bench** or piece of **garden sculpture**. An ideal labor-saving device as well as useful and/or great to look at and break the ice in any conversation!

Create lots of **color** in the garden by painting pots, fences, garden furniture etc. This will liven up the garden without any planting and will also look cheerful in the winter.

If **gaps** appear between paving slabs, refill them by brushing in dry mortar. Never do this job when the paving is wet or the mortar may stain the surface.

To protect your arms when pruning or hedging cut the top and bottom off of a large plastic bottle and use as sleeves, no more scratches.

You can put pots inside the window box instead of filling the box with soil. This allows you to lift them out and change them around without disturbing the roots. It also reduces the weight of the window box. Make sure both have drainage holes otherwise the plants will become waterlogged.

Choose low growing plants for your **window box** if you want maximum light from your window. Climbers are another option as they can be trained against the wall around the window.

Always **wipe tools** with an oily rag before putting them away to keep them in good order for next time.

To **save buying hanging baskets** every few years spray or paint new ones with 3 coats of yacht varnish to protect them. They will last 3 times longer.

Window boxes should be at least 200mm (8 ins) deep to allow for root growth and to prevent soil drying out too quickly.

Feast on Flowers
A lot of flowers can be eaten but never use flowers that have been sprayed with pesticides, those from the florists usually have been - and make absolutely certain that they are edible.

Dip elderflowers in a light batter and deep-fry them. Serve with cinnamon sugar and some chilled crème fraiche. They also make great cordial: dig out your old recipe books and get bottling.

Hawthorn or May has young leaf buds that can be cooked or thrown raw into salads and the haws or berries can be made into a relish or jellies. Dog-rose petals can be used to flavour apple jelly, and they give a delicious perfume when added to salads.

Store **edible flowers** in an airtight box in the fridge for anything up to a week. And don't let all those flavoursome herbs go to waste either.

Sesame seeds contain a compound called sesamol which can stop the growth of cancer cells.

Gardening for only **20 minutes a day** or spending a little time in your local park benefits your health. Exposure to plants gives benefits including reduced risk of coronary heart disease, better concentration and lower stress levels.

Strawberries are a top source of **vitamin C**, having more than oranges. Victorian women tried bathing in strawberries so as to enlarge their breasts.

Need a windbreak in the garden? High fencing can and some structures

can be expensive. Our idea is to have a **natural & movable windbreak.**
This can contain, runner beans, sweetpeas or any climbers or creepers of
your choice. If choosing sweet peas then make sure the box is at least 12"
deep, sweet peas like to be planted deep. The oblong box can be made out
of old sleepers, planks or any old fencing etc. lying around. The oblong
box can be as long or short as you wish.

Screw a castor at each corner of the bottom. Use old buggy, pram or old
furniture castors. Make a couple of holes in the bottom for drainage and
put some gravel or crocks in the bottom. Fill with compost and put some
poles, or bamboo at quite close intervals. Make sure these are secure, put
lots of pebbles or stones around the base at earth level. Place a plant of
your choice next to each pole and wait to grow. As the plants wind
themselves up and around each pole it will develop into a natural wind
brake and can also be moved to wherever you choose to sit in the garden.

Those who contemplate the beauty of the earth find
reserves of strength that will endure as long as life lasts.

Rachel Carson

THE CHEAP LAZY GARDENER
HAS THE LAST LAUGH

Basic Philosophy - Gardening Rule:
When weeding, the best way to make sure you are removing a weed and not a valuable plant is to pull on it. If it comes out of the ground easily, it is a valuable plant.

NOT Voltaire...
A beautiful woman loved growing tomatoes, but couldn't seem to get her tomatoes to turn red. One day while taking a stroll she came upon a gentleman neighbour who had the most beautiful garden full of huge red tomatoes. The woman asked the gentleman: "What do you do to get your tomatoes so red?"
The gentleman responded: "Well twice a day I stand in front of my tomato garden and expose myself, and the tomatoes turn red from blushing so much". The woman was so impressed; she decided to try doing the same thing to her tomato garden to see if it would work.
So twice a day for two weeks she exposed herself to her garden hoping for the best.
One day the gentleman was passing by and asked the woman: "By the way, how did you make out?" "Did your tomatoes turn red?"
"No" she replied: "But my cucumbers are enormous".

Eight Things not to say when visiting a Garden Centre
• Have you anything pink that grows to about 9".
• We tried it in the front and then in the back it seemed better when we had it on the patio.
• My next-door neighbour liked it so much, when it got big enough my husband poked it through the fence into next doors garden. They were ever so grateful.
• We were told it was hardy but it shrivelled in the winter.
• Have you got anything to stop wind?
• We can't do it now it's the wrong time of the month.
• My husband works away and I want him to put it in before he goes.
• We had it last year and I didn't like it so we are not trying it again.

The world is a rose; smell it and pass it to your friends.

Persian Proverb

CHEAP LAZY BIRTHDAY FLOWERS

Most of us know that we have a birthstone designated to each month of the year but did you know that each month has a flower assigned to it?

We have listed both your birthstone with its flower.

January   Flower: Carnation
              Birthstone: Garnet

February   Flower: Violet
              Birthstone: Amethyst

March   Flower: Jonquil
              Birthstone: Aquamarine

April   Flower: Sweet Pea
              Birthstone: Diamond

May   Flower: Lily of the Valley
              Birthstone: Emerald

June   Flower: Rose
              Birthstone: Pearl

July   Flower: Larkspur
              Birthstone: Ruby

August   Flower: Gladiolus
              Birthstone: Peridot

September   Flower: Aster
              Birthstone: Sapphire

October   Flower: Calendula
              Birthstone: Opal

November   Flower: Chrysanthemum
              Birthstone: Topaz

December   Flower: Narcissus
              Birthstone: Turquoise

It is at the edge of a petal that love waits.

William Carlos Williams

CHEAP LAZY PLANT SPELLS AND LOVE POTIONS

There are a thousand and one gypsy fortune tellers out there longing to take your money to solve your problems. Psychics and witches abound offering cast iron guarantees that their spells will work for you.

There are two main things to bear in mind. The first is that the cosmos never rewards those who force things as they might expect and desire. It never, ever works. No matter how much you may long to manipulate matters to "bring back Brian" or "make Alicia love me", unless that is the best solution all round it won't come about. The best you can ask for is "please bring me my heart's desire, or something better that is right for me".

The second is that you are your own best magician. Others can help of course, to a degree. But always check out the credentials of anyone who asks you for money under any guise. They will be serving their own best interests, not yours.

Here are some free "helping hands" that are fun to try.
Your garden is full of all sorts of protective remedies. For example:

African Ginger	Use to protect against evil spirits and hexes, spread around your house.
Angelica Root	Place over the door to protect your house.
Anise	Said to increase psychic abilities when taken as a tea.
Brimstone	Burn outside your home to dispel demons.
Buckeye	Said to attract money to the business or home.
Catnip	Place about the home for power and love.
Comfrey	Said to protect the traveller.
Cowslip	Place in a doorway to prevent unwanted visitors.
Couch Grass	Use to attract a new lover.

Fennel Seeds	Carry in you pocket or bag to prevent negativity.
Flax	Use in tea to enhance psychic abilities.
Holy Thistle	Use to enhance spiritual help.
Hyssop	Use for purification of any space.
Kava Kava Root	Protection whilst travelling and from accidents.
Lavender	Use to promote love
Peony root	Use as a lucky charm.
Queen of the Meadow	Bathe in it to see your future.
Asparagus	Rich in Vitamin E, thought to stimulate hormones for a healthy sex life.
Chile Peppers	Raises your pulse, triggers endorphins to give you a natural high.
Chocolate	Everyone's favourite! Contains the "love chemical" stimulant phenylethylamine.
Damiana	Traditional aphrodisiac, can increase genital sensitivity and maybe erotic dreams!

To check if the man of your dreams is truly yours, offer him a sprig of **basil**. If he accepts it, then he is yours.

If you would like to marry, place a **bay leaf** under your pillow on St. Valentine's day. Whisper softly: "St. Valentine, be kind to me; in my dreams let me my true love see." If you dream of love, you will marry within the year.

Open your heart and that of your lover by blending essential oil of **ylang ylang** plus r**ose, ladies mantle** and **lavender** in equal portions (a few drops of each) and adding to a pure carrier oil to dilute (about 1 percent).

Try combining half a teaspoon of your essential oil blend to half a cup of sweet almond oil to make a good massage oil.

For loving kindness with strength and endurance, blend 3 drops of essential oil of tuberose with one drop each of **pink pepper, rose** and **plumeria.**

For attraction, combine 3 drops each of **patchouli** and **lavender** with 1 drop of **cedarwood.**

For romance, add 4 drops of rose to 2 drops of **gardenia** and 1 drop of **lavender.**

For true love, combine 3 drops of rose, 2 drops of **sandalwood**, 2 drops of **jasmine** 1 drop of **heiliotrope** and 1 drop of **ylang ylang.**

To ensure your lover is faithful to you forever, plant marigolds on the ground where he walks.

The scent of **licorice** is supposed to be arousing for women, and **popcorn** and **pumpkin pie** for men.

For long term fidelity, share **periwinkle leaves** with your partner.

WICCA INCANTATION
Bide the Wiccan law ye must,
In perfect love, in perfect trust.
Eight words the Wiccan Rede fulfil,
And harm ye none, do what ye will.
What ye send forth comes back to thee,
So ever mind the rule of three.
Follow ye this with mind and heart,
So merry ye meet, and merry part.

Love is the only flower that grows and blossoms without the aid of the seasons.

Kahlil Gibran

LOVE POTION TEA

2 teaspoons of rose conjou tea, or a good assam
3 pinches of thyme and 3 of nutmeg
1 pinch of rosemary
4 leaves of fresh mint
7 fresh rose petals
7 lemon leaves
3 cups of spring water
1/2 a teaspoon of organic honey

Brew this tea during the time of a waxing moon, on a Friday, while chanting:

"By the light of the (January) moon waxing I brew this tea
To make (Harry) my lover desire me."

Insert appropriate month and lover's name.
Drink the tea and chant:

"Goddess of love, hear my plea, let (Harry) my lover desire me,
So let it be, so let it be."

The next Friday, brew up another pot of tea as above and serve to your proposed lover. If the omens are favourable he or she will very shortly fall in love with you.

A morning glory at my window satisfies me more than the metaphysics of books.
Walt Whitman

LOVE POTION NUMBER 9

The Searcher's song title is re-emerging in all sorts of beauty products and scents. Charmed World's perfumed body oil ($14 for 2 oz from Beautyjungle.com) shares the name with Penhaligon's line of cologne ($22 for 0.05 fluid oz), link enamel cuff links ($270) and a scented pen for ecstatic love lines ($70) at Saks Fifth Avenue and outlets in other countries.

A rocket No. 9 recipe for love is as follows:

9 oz of red wine

9 red rose petals

9 cloves

9 drops apple juice

9 drops vanilla extract

9 strawberries, pureed

1 ginseng root, cut into 9 equal portions

9 seeds from a red apple and 9 pomegranate seeds

Light 9 red candles and place these 9 ingredients into a pot at the 9th hour of the 9th day of the 9th month. Stir the potion clockwise 9 times with an olive wood spoon while chanting:

"Let the man/woman who drinks this wine

Shower me with love divine

Sweet love potion number 9

Make his/her love forever mine."

Bring the mix to the boil, then reduce the heat and simmer for 9 minutes. Remove it from the heat and let cool. Blow on the potion 9 times, each time blessing it in the name of one of the 9 goddesses of love: Ishtar, Astarte, Inanna, Aphrodite, Venus, Nephthys, Hathor, Arianrhod, Freya, and then strain through a fine cheesecloth into a clean new container. Cover and refrigerate, keeping it aside to serve only to the one whom you desire to love you, ensuring that they alone see it, touch it or drink it.

LOVERS' BATH SALTS

Combine 1 cup of epsom salts, 1 cup sea salt and 2 teaspoons of finely ground oatmeal, 1 teaspoon bicarbonate of soda, 1 teaspoon of cinnamon, 1 teaspoon of ginger, 1/2 teaspoon of cloves with 4 drops of essential oil of patchouli in a beautiful new container. Use a different essential oil if desired (ie. rose, jasmine, lavender, cedarwood, orange, sandalwood). Add to bathwater as desired.

LOVERS CHAMPAGNE COCKTAILS

Passion By Moonlight
1/4 cup Chinese ginger liqueur
1/4 cup freshly squeezed orange juice
1/4 cup Fentiman's ginger beer
1/2 teaspoon minced fresh ginger

Stir together. Add 1 part of the above mix to 3 parts Charles Heidsick champagne. Serve in Dartford crystal champagne glasses.

Paris in the Spring
Take 4 fresh ripe organic white peaches and puree
Mix in 4 teaspoons of Remy Martin brandy

Stir together. Add 1 part of the mix to 3 parts Laurent Perrier champagne. Serve in Waterford crystal champagne glasses with a lump of sugar in each glass.

Two websites with free readings are:
www.micheleknight.com and www.astro-service.com.

Flowers are love's truest language.
Park Benjamin

BIBIOLGRAPHY

Boland, Maureen and Bridget, Old Wives' Lore for Gardeners, The Bodley Head Ltd., London, 1976

Chopra, Deepak, The Book of Secrets, Rider, Ebury Press, Random House, London, 2004

Cooper, Diana, A Little Light On Angels, Findhorn Press, 1996

Hellyer, A.G.L., The Amateur Gardener, Collingridge Books, Hamlyn Publishing Group, London, 1977

Hessayon, Dr. D.G., The Easy-Care Gardening Expert , Expert Books, Transworld Publishers, London, 2004

Hunt, Peter, Ed. Gardening For All, Octopus Books Ltd., London, 1986

Marshall Cavendish, Grow Your Own, 52 weekly parts, London, 1977

Neylon, Margaret, Angel Magic, Element, Harper Collins Publishers, London , 2001

Philip. Neil, Ed. Best Loved Poems, Little, Brown and Company, London, 2002

Raven, Sarah, The Great Vegetable Plot, BBC Books, London, 2005

White, Ruth, Working With Guides and Angels, Piatkus Books Ltd., London, 1996

Wilson, Paul, Instant Calm, Penguin Books, London,1995

Wydra, Nancilee, Feng Shui, The Book Of Cures, Contemporary Books, NTC/ Contemporary Publishing Company, Lincolnwood, Illinois, USA, 1996

Selected Other Sources:

Chiswick Horticultural and Allotments Society
www.links2love.com
www.allfreecrafts.com
www.louepicure.com
www.swfwmd.state.fl.us
www.starchefs.com
www.digsmagazine.com.
www.carryongardening.org.uk
www.gardening-tips-perennials.com
www.kidsgardening.com
www.bbc.co.uk